W9-DIO-193

KING COAL

A Pictorial Heritage of West Virginia Coal Mining

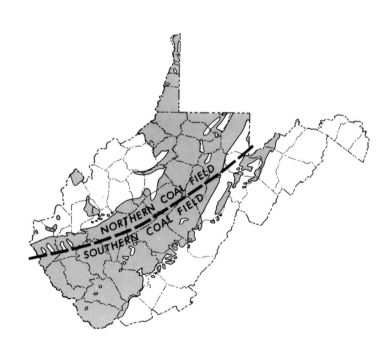

KING COAL

A Pictorial Heritage of West Virginia Coal Mining

By Stan Cohen

QUARRIER PRESS
CHARLESTON, WEST VIRGINIA

©1984 STAN COHEN
(All rights reserved by Quarrier Press, L.L.C.)

No part of this book may be reproduced in any form
or in any means, electronic or mechanical,
including photocopying, recording,
or by any information storage and retrieval system,
without permission in writing from the publisher.

Library of Congress Number: 84-61934
ISBN 1-891852-06-X
(Formerly ISBN 0-933126-53-0)

Eleventh Printing: June 1999

Printed in the United States of America

Typography: Arrow Graphics
Cover Art: Monte Dolack

Distributed by:
Pictorial Histories Distribution
1416 Quarrier Street
Charleston, WV 25301

TABLE OF CONTENTS

A large seam of coal exposed by strip mining, Nicholas County, 1955. *U.S. Forest Service*

INTRODUCTION

No STATE in the Union has been more dominated by one product or natural resource than has West Virginia. Since the beginnings of coal mining in the early 1800s, the economy, welfare, and political life of West Virginia have been largely dependent upon its "black gold," that underlies a great portion of the state.

Coal was not a very important resource in West Virginia until after the Civil War. It was then that the advent of the railroads made the coalfields accessible and brought thousands of miners into the state. Since then, West Virginia has been fertile ground for outside exploitation, massive labor confrontations, union organizing, and a multitude of political intrigues. The coalfields have provided great wealth to individuals and corporations, while many of the miners and their families have known equally great poverty. West Virginians have seen their state's landscape altered by underground mining and more recently by the impact of strip mining. The state's economy has been buffeted by the up-and-down cycles brought on by the price and use of "King Coal."

The story of coal mining in West Virginia is a fascinating one that has been well documented through the years in numerous books and articles. The story, however, has never been portrayed adequately in pictures. This book will attempt to explore pictorially the history of underground coal mining in West Virginia, both the good and the bad, and show how this mineral has affected the history and development of the state. The reader who is interested in a more detailed history will find the more recent publications on the subject listed in the bibliography.

The photographs used were selected from a number of sources both within and outside of the state's boundaries. There are thousands of photos available; I have tried to choose a few hundred from these that are most representative of coal mining's story. As more photographs come to light, additions and corrections can be made in future reprints.

This book could not have been written without the excellent cooperation of many individuals in West Virginia. I wish to thank the staffs of the West Virginia State Archives in Charleston and the West Virginia University Archives in Morgantown, where the bulk of the photographs were obtained. I would also like to thank the staff of the Craft Memorial Library, Bluefield, for allowing me access to the vast Pocahontas Fuel Collection. The staff members of the West Virginia Department of Mines and the West Virginia Geological and Economic Survey were also helpful with information, as were Don Page of the Beckley Exhibition Coal Mine, and Gene Cox of the National Park Service, New River Gorge National River. In addition, a special thanks to Mike Meador of Athens, Dick Fauss of Charleston, Richard and Doug Andre of Charleston, and Ken Sullivan of *Goldenseal* magazine for their help and encouragement. Eugenia Thoenen of Charleston edited the manuscript, and Monte Dolack designed the cover illustration.

Stan Cohen
November 1984

PHOTO CREDITS

WVU—West Virginia University Archives, Morgantown
SWV—West Virginia State Archives, Charleston
NPS—National Park Service, New River Gorge National River, Oak Hill
LC—Library of Congress, Washington, D.C.
NA—National Archives, Washington, D.C.
Other photographs are acknowledged to the source, or taken by the author

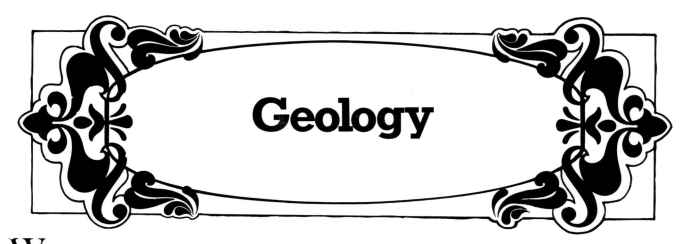

Geology

WEST VIRGINIA has been blessed with as great a concentration of a natural resource as any state in this country. Coal occurs in fifty-three of the fifty-five counties; only Jefferson and Hardy counties are completely barren. Forty-three counties have deposits of economic importance, and approximately thirty-five have mined or are currently mining coal.

When mining began in the early 1800s, the estimate of minable coal was a staggering total of approximately 117 billion tons. Of this, about 100 billion tons remain in sixty-two minable and fifty-five unminable seams. It is presently estimated that at today's rate of production, five hundred years of coal production are left. Adding this to the reserves of bituminous and lower-grade coals in the other states, the United States has a tremendous fuel reserve still locked in its land.

Dr. Israel C. White, the first state geologist, reported on the status of coal in the state in the Geological Survey's 1903 *Coal Report:*

> Those who seek gold, silver, copper, tin, lead, and other costly metals, should waste no time in West Virginia. Traces she may have of all, but none in commercial quantity . . . But while precious stones, gems, and metals, have been denied the Little Mountain State, yet generous nature has so richly endowed her with common minerals that her natural wealth is unsurpassed by any equal area on the continent. These are some of her riches . . . clays, shales, and silica beds . . . limestones . . . building stones . . . natural gas fields . . . and last but not least, *coal* in great variety and quantity. (Italics added.)

Most people think of coal only as a black rock; its formation, however, has many steps, and it takes thousands of years through geologic time to develop. In its simplest form coal is in the sedimentary rock family with sandstone, shale, and limestone. The difference is that coal is derived from the decay of plant life rather than from clay or sand particles, or chemical compounds. It is actually an organic rock, akin to petroleum and natural gas in its natural state.

Coal's origins are the remains of plants that once grew in coal swamps. These swamps, which at various times covered most of the state, were a vast depository of plants that decomposed in the stagnant water as they died. Because of the low oxygen content in the swamps, the plants were incompletely decomposed by the microscopic decay organisms. This partially decomposed material formed what are now known as peat bogs.

Under increased heat and pressure resulting from the successive layering of sandstone, shale, and limestone deposited on top, the peat underwent progressive chemical and physical alterations. As more sediments covered the material, the peat eventually underwent lithification, or hardening, into rock.

Geologists place the beginnings of the Coal Age about 315 million years ago, at the start of what is known in geologic time as the Pennsylvanian Period. This, together with the earlier Mississippian Period, make up the Carboniferous Age. The first Coal Age lasted for approximately 45 million years, until the early part of the Permian Period.

Almost all the valuable coal seams were laid during the Pennsylvanian Period, in-

Coal Measures plants.

Cordaites

Calamites.

Sigillaria

Lepidodendron

cluding the deposits stretching from the Canadian Maritime Provinces south to Alabama, generally paralleling the Appalachian Mountain chain. At that time the entire area must have been a single, broad, flat plain very close to sea level, periodically covered with a single vast swamp or an interconnected series of lesser ones. Between the intervals during which these swamps covered the land's surface, sea waters and river-mouth deltas alternately swept back and forth over the region, depositing an immense amount of sediment over the swamps. In this battle between land and sea, the sea ultimately lost.

Physical characteristics of coal are varied. Rank is the term used to express the relative proportion of fixed carbon in the coal, i.e., the percentage of nonvolatile carbon and carbon compounds. With continuing heat and pressure, called metamorphism, the volatile material is driven off, and the rank increases. When all the volatile material is gone, the end product is graphite. Bituminous coal, which is found in West Virginia, has a rank below that of anthracite, which is the highest form of coal.

Other impurities in coal include sulphur and ash. Sulphur occurs in several different forms. Ash includes all the noncombustible matter such as silt, sand, clay, and the chemical compounds of calcium and iron.

Coal beds in the state generally are flat-lying and vary in thickness from a few inches to many feet. The great Pittsburgh seam has been measured at over 12 feet in some locations. At least 30 inches of thickness is the general rule for a workable coal seam. Beds of clay or shale, called partings, separate the coal. A bed of clay called underclay or fineclay is usually underneath the coal; roof shale, which is a fine-grained rock of either shale or siltstone, rests on top. It is often called slate by the miners.

Two special varieties of coal that commonly occur are known as cannel and bone, both of which exhibit a dull luster rather than the bright one of bituminous coal. Cannel has a conchoidal fracture. It breaks along curved surfaces like glass and consists almost entirely of millions of spores, or pollen grains, produced by Coal Age plants. Bone is coal with a very high ash content. It is not a commercial product.

The overall geologic setting for the coal measures in the state is shown in Figure One. An imaginary hinge line basically separates the coal deposits into northern and southern coalfields. In general the coal in the northern fields has a higher sulphur content than that in the southern fields.

Coal has its place in the geologic time table like other rock formations; as we have seen, most of the West Virginia coal falls into the Pennsylvania and early Permian periods. The older coals of the southern coalfields are higher in overall quality. In the *History of the West Virginia Coal Industry,* by Phil Conley, the reader will find a detailed history of the ten distinct coalfields located in the state: Kanawha, Fairmont, Elkins, New River, Flat-Top, Pocahontas, Winding Gulf, Logan, Williamson, Greenbrier, and Northern Panhandle. The major portion of the original coal reserves lies in the southern fields. The bulk of West Virginia coal, therefore, is high-quality bituminous.

Coal Producing Counties in West Virginia. *Courtesy of the West Virginia Geological and Economic Survey.*

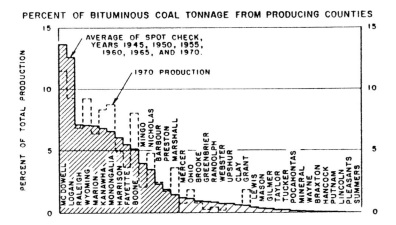

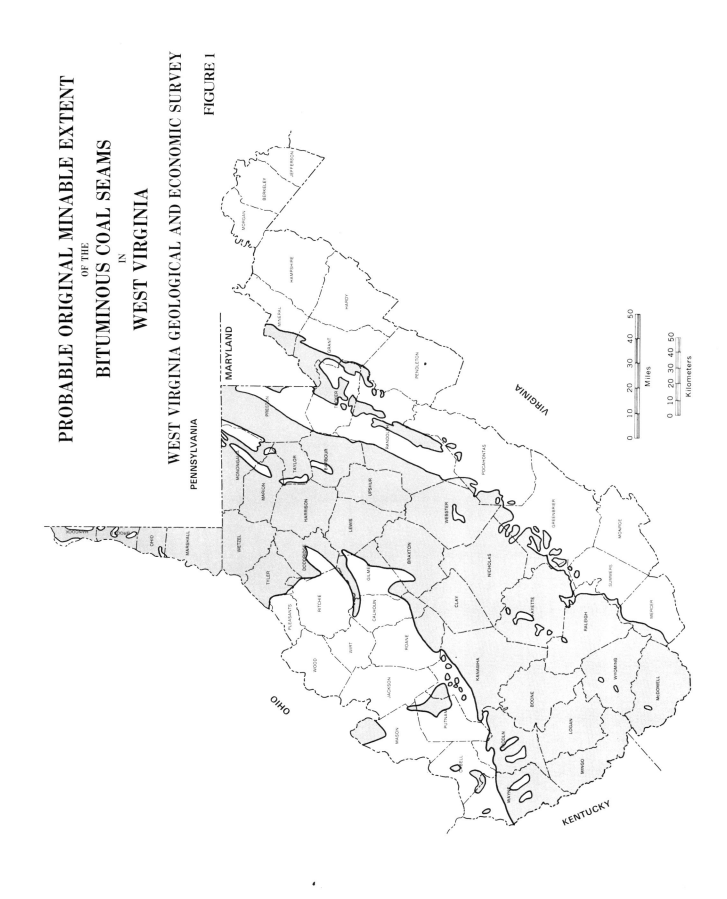

PROBABLE ORIGINAL MINABLE EXTENT
OF THE
BITUMINOUS COAL SEAMS
IN
WEST VIRGINIA

WEST VIRGINIA GEOLOGICAL AND ECONOMIC SURVEY

FIGURE 1

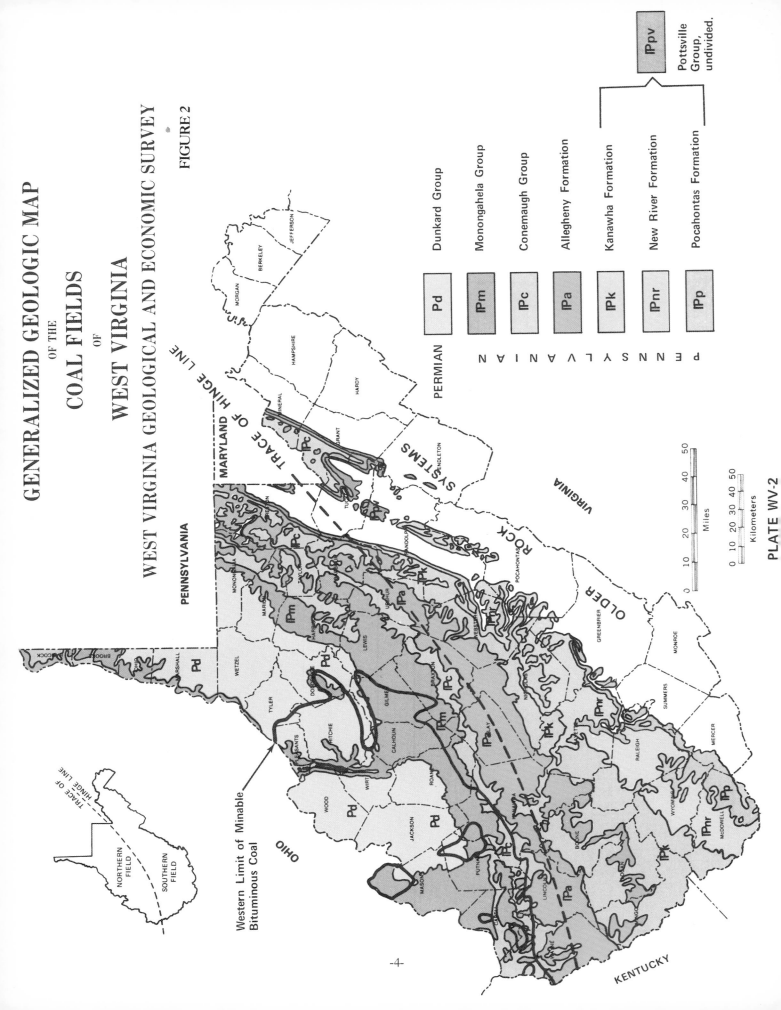

GENERALIZED GEOLOGIC MAP

OF THE

COAL FIELDS
OF
WEST VIRGINIA

WEST VIRGINIA GEOLOGICAL AND ECONOMIC SURVEY

FIGURE 2

PLATE WV-2

PERMIAN

Pd	Dunkard Group

PENNSYLVANIAN

ℙm	Monongahela Group
ℙc	Conemaugh Group
ℙa	Allegheny Formation
ℙk	Kanawha Formation
ℙnr	New River Formation
ℙp	Pocahontas Formation
ℙpv	Pottsville Group, undivided.

Western Limit of Minable Bituminous Coal

TRACE OF HINGE LINE

NORTHERN FIELD

SOUTHERN FIELD

MARYLAND

PENNSYLVANIA

OHIO

KENTUCKY

VIRGINIA

YOUNGER SYSTEMS ROCK OLDER

0 10 20 30 40 50 Miles

0 10 20 30 40 50 Kilometers

-4-

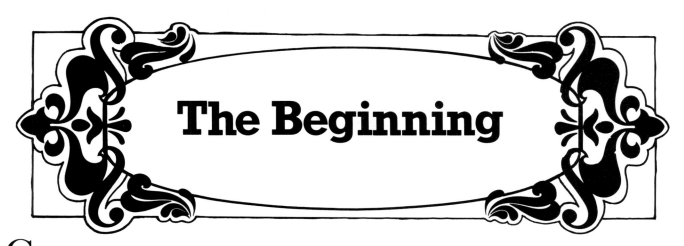

The Beginning

COAL WAS FIRST noted in North America by Father Louis Hennipin on a journey down the Illinois River in 1679. John Peter Salley of Augusta County, Virginia, is credited with the first discovery of coal in what is now West Virginia. Salley was on an exploratory trip across the Allegheny Mountains in 1742 when he came to a small stream in the Kanawha Valley. There the exploring party found "a large plenty of coals, for which we named it Coal River." (The site is now located in Boone County.)

Nothing was done with this discovery, however, until the early 1800s, when the manufacture of salt became a big business in the Kanawha Valley. For years wood was used in the process of drying out the salt brine which was pumped from wells, but with increased production the wood supply was soon exhausted. Coal, which was plentiful in the surrounding hills, was used as a substitute as early as 1817.

During the years preceding the Civil War, coal became more of an economic factor in the valley, and the first commercial coal company was incorporated on March 10, 1834. Slaves were even brought to some areas to mine the resource. Coal was shipped

Coal mining in the 1800s was back-breaking work performed often by single men in many small coal mines, providing the product mainly for local consumption. SWV via New York Public Library

down the Kanawha River during periods of high water to Cincinnati and occasionally to markets as far south as New Orleans.

An 1836 state geological report by Professor William B. Rogers of the University of Virginia painted a glowing picture of the potential for coal development in the Kanawha Valley. Shortly thereafter out-of-state and foreign investors came into the valley, buying stock in the various locally owned coal companies or founding their own.

Coal production in the valley was greatly expanded by the discovery of the means of extracting kerosene from cannel coal, a variety of which there were large deposits in the region. Until the discovery of underground oil reserves in Pennsylvania in 1859, cannel-coal oil was a substantial growth industry.

Transportation was a serious problem for the coal industry until the 1870s, when the Chesapeake and Ohio Railway finally laid its rails across the Alleghenies and down the Kanawha Valley to the Ohio River at Huntington. This opened up markets both east and west, and dozens of coal companies were subsequently formed. Branch lines snaked out into the previously isolated sections of Boone, Clay, Putnam, Fayette, and Braxton counties.

The saltworks in the Kanawha Valley were the impetus for the beginnings of large-scale coal mining in the area in the early 1800s. As timber supplies diminished for heating the salt brine, coal took wood's place. *SWV*

In the northern part of the state, coal was sighted as early as 1790, but there was no mention of shipments until 1835. Professor Rogers also visited this region, again extolling the virtues of the new mineral. The thick Pittsburgh coal seam, prominent in northern West Virginia, assured the area of a steady growth in coal production as transportation methods improved.

Mines were operating in the Fairmont region by 1850 for local consumption. When the Baltimore and Ohio Railroad reached Fairmont in 1853, markets opened up as far east as Baltimore. The coalfields around Wheeling, in the Northern Panhandle, were also mined prior to the Civil War; the coal was needed for a fledgling iron industry in that city that had begun before the War of 1812. The Baltimore and Ohio reached Wheeling in the early 1850s, providing access to eastern markets.

The northern coalfields assumed greater importance during the Civil War, when supplies from Virginia were cut off. The larger cities of the East needed a steady supply of coal for heating purposes and war-related industries. Union forces were able to keep the Baltimore and Ohio and the Northwestern railroads open to Washington, D.C., and Baltimore, notwithstanding constant raids by the Confederates from 1861 to 1865. The end of the war saw the expansion of coal mining in Marion, Taylor, Preston, Monongalia, Barbour, and Harrison counties.

An additional area of early coal mining was located in the Eastern Panhandle. In 1798 coal was shipped from Mineral and Berkeley counties to the government arsenal at Harpers Ferry. This region also became a source of coal for the East during the Civil War. One of the first coal barons, Henry Gassaway Davis, got his start in the Eastern Panhandle. As more railroads were completed in the late 1800s and early 1900s, coalfields in Grant, Randolph, Tucker, Upshur, and Webster counties were opened.

The remainder of West Virginia's coalfields, those in the southern counties of Logan, Mingo, McDowell, Wyoming, Mercer, Wayne and Summers, had to wait for the coming of the railroads to that section in the late nineteenth century to realize their vast potential.

This early scene, perhaps from the 1870s, shows fifteen-ton drop-bottom railroad cars called hoppers at the Gaston Gas Coal Company. The Gaston mine was located on the West Fork River in northern West Virginia and operated from 1875 until 1925. The coal was shipped via the Baltimore and Ohio Railroad to markets in the East. *WVU*

Housing for miners in the southern coalfields in the 1880s was quite primitive, even by the standards of the day. Thousands of European immigrants and blacks from the South poured into the state when the railroads opened up the vast coal tracts for exploration and mining. *WVU*

One of the first tipples in the Pocahontas coalfields, erected at the mine of the Mill Creek Coal & Coke Company in 1885. Beneath the tipple can be seen what is now the eastern entrance of the Norfolk and Western Railway Coaldale Tunnel. *WVU*

Temporary tipple at the Louisville Coal & Coke Company, Mercer County, circa 1880s. *WVU*

This remarkable photo shows an early loading dock at the mouth of a mine. The small wooden coal cars are pulled by dogs. The horse-drawn wagons were pulled up underneath, and the contents of the mine cars were dumped into them. Apparently coal was also stored in the bins below; perhaps there were screens to sort the coal either in wagons or in the bins. *WVU*

Miners at work at Crumpler, McDowell County, in 1904. These could have been some of the first electric locomotives. Notice the miners' homes scattered on the hillside. *WVU*

Mining Methods* and Operations

COMMERCIAL COAL mining in the state began around 1817. From that time until the 1930s, the production of coal was accomplished for the most part by hand labor. In the beginning of the industry, coal was mined primarily for local consumption. The mines were small, operated by a family or a few men. Before the Civil War, slave labor was sometimes used. The earliest mining method was simply to open a drift in the hillside, dig away at the coal with a pick, load up a basket or cart, and haul it to the opening.

Coal seams could vary in thickness from two to twelve feet. This fact, along with the topographical location of the seam, regulated the type and ease of mining. A deep seam required a shaft entrance, a seam close to the surface necessitated a slope entry, and a seam that could be entered from a hillside had a drift entry. Most of the early mines used the latter for easy entry; with drifting, the miners could walk to work, and complex hoisting machinery was not needed.

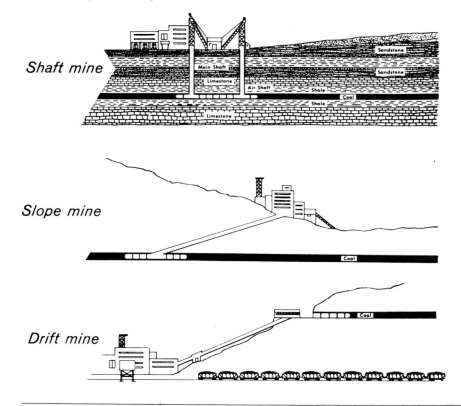

Shaft mine

Slope mine

Drift mine

*Portions of this chapter were taken from *The Mining Life: Coal in Our History and Culture*, an exhibition sponsored by the Humanities Foundation of West Virginia, the National Endowment for the Humanities, the West Virginia Department of Culture and History, and the Claude Benedum Foundation.

When coal was dug and loaded by hand, the miner's work area was referred to as his "place." The place was a narrow tunnel, the height of which usually paralleled that of the coal seam on which the miner was working. Because of this, the miner could rarely stand upright. The roof was supported by blocks of coal called pillars that were left in place for this purpose. While the miner dug at one end of the tunnel (the face), narrow-gauge track to accomodate the cars that hauled coal to the surface was laid in the open end.

The first step in digging out the coal consisted of undercutting the coal face. A three- or four-foot-deep slit called the kerf was made at the bottom of the seam. A piece of wood known as a sprag was placed under the kerf to keep the coal from falling until the miner was ready. Undercutting could take from 2 to 6½ hours a day depending on the miner's abilities, the width of the room, and the hardness of the coal.

Holes for the blasting powder were drilled following the completion of the undercutting. The miner used a five- or six-foot-long breast auger to drill a hole of the right depth and angle for the powder, an extremely dangerous substance to handle. When the explosive was set, the hole was carefully corked with clay or dirt with the use of a tamping rod and needle; the latter stayed in contact with the powder when the rod was withdrawn. When the needle was removed, it left a small tunnel in the powder that was the proper size for the fuse (squib). The fuse was then lit, the miner taking shelter behind one of the pillars.

Taken from W.P. Tams', *The Smokeless Coalfields of West Virginia*, Morgantown, 1963.

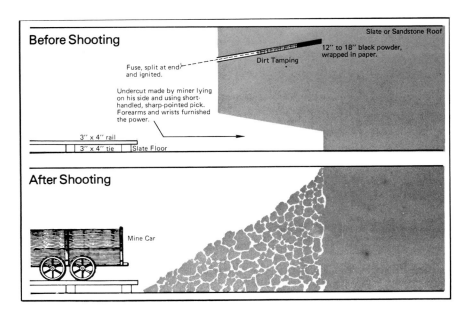

Shot down coal at a working coal face. *WVU*

Boring a hole for blasting powder by hand auger, Crozier Coal and Coke Company, Elkhorn, McDowell County. *N&W Railway*

The fallen coal was shoveled into one of the empty mine cars, a difficult job, especially in low seams. While loading the coal, the miner had to remove the larger pieces of shale and rock so he would not be docked for sending out "dirty" coal. Lump coal sold at a premium price; pea-sized or slack coal was not so desirable. The miner hung a brass "check" on each car he loaded in order to get proper credit for the coal he dug. In the mid-1920s, a miner could mine and load more than ten tons of coal a day.

At first the miner would haul the coal back to the surface himself, but soon companies used mules or other animals such as horses, oxen, and even dogs for this purpose. Small "gathering" locomotives were introduced at a later date.

The room and pillar system of mining coal described above has always been the most common one used. Tunnels, or entries, are dug into the coal seam from the mine opening. Side entries are then driven off the main entry about every four hundred feet. They run approximately twelve to fifteen hundred feet and block out a rectangular panel of coal. Each panel is then divided into twenty or so rooms, which are dug at right angles to the side entries. Most mining activity occurs in the rooms.

Two parallel entries are always driven into the coal seam to control the current of air. Crosscuts between the two entries provide ventilation, crucial to the safety of any mining operation.

An early mining car.

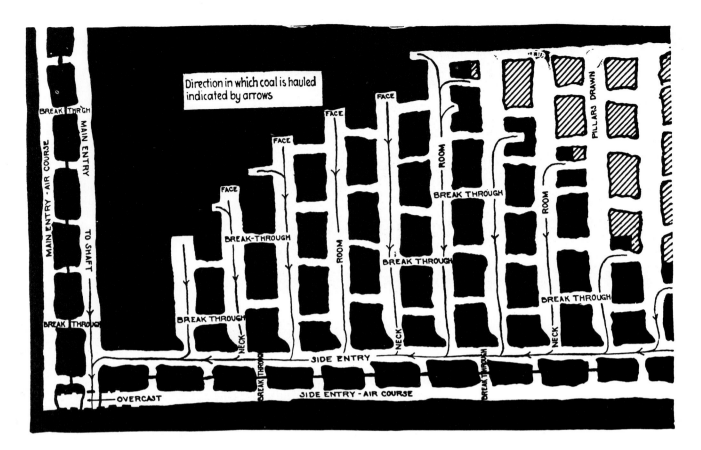

Map of a portion of a working panel showing the location of the main entry, side entry, working rooms and the face. Shaded area indicates that pillar removal is in progress, while the arrows show the direction in which the coal is being hauled.

A young mule driver. Notice the whip around his neck and his primitive miner's lamp. *SWV*

In the early days of the mining industry, a miner learned how to mine by experience. He would work with another miner until he felt confident enough to work at a face alone. The early miner performed all mining tasks himself, including laying track for the coal cars, loading the cars, supporting the roof, and even hauling the loaded cars to the mine entrance, as noted previously. As production increased and companies grew, however, systems involving a division of labor were instituted. Each miner having a specific task to perform gave the companies more control over their labor force.

Young boys often went into the mines with their fathers to learn the trade. They were given odd jobs at first, such as door-tending, or "trapping," which consisted of sitting near a ventilation door and opening it as the mule drivers, or "skinners," passed with their loads of coal. Another, more dangerous job was spragging, stopping a runaway coal car by sticking a short, round, tapered piece of wood into the spokes of its wheels. By the end of World War I, however, the employment of children had virtually been outlawed.

One source of constant tension between miners and coal companies was the matter of fair payment for a load of coal. "Shortweighing," practiced by some unscrupulous companies to cheat their miners, occurred when the company weighman would record a weight less than the actual amount in the car. "Dockage" was an arbitrary reduction in payment for impurities loaded in the coal car; usually more was docked than should have been.

These practices became so commonplace that one of the first demands of the miners when the union was formed was for their own check-weighman to monitor the company weighman. The miners felt that only with such a system would they be paid a fair amount for the coal they sent to the surface.

Hand loading coal was
a difficult job, especially
in low-seam coal.
National Coal Association

Loading coal by hand.
WVU

Checking for gas in the
mine. *WVU*

For many years animals were used to haul the loaded coal cars to the surface. Oxen, horses, mules and even dogs were used. Some of these animals were kept underground for years, and underground stables were constructed for them. Gradually electric locomotives phased out the use of these beasts of burden. *NPS; WVU; SWV*

A track crew laying rails inside a mine. In the early days miners usually had to lay their own track to their working face; later the companies established greater job specifications to obtain increased efficiency. *WVU*

A typical coal-mine haulage way. *NA*

An early engineering/survey team in the southern coalfields, 1902. *SWV*

A fifteen-year-old "trapper." Children were hired for a few cents a day to open and close doors for coal cars ready for unloading. Child labor laws were finally passed in the early part of the twentieth century. *NA*

Everything in these photographs—the wooden mine supports, the open flame, the soft hats and shoes, and the shovel—are now obsolete. *National Coal Association*

Setting a mine timber. *WVU*

-19-

The late 1800s saw the first advances toward mechanization of the coal industry. Internal-combustion engines were tried briefly but abandoned for use underground. The danger of fire was too great from the engines and the fumes they emitted too toxic. The earliest successful attempts at mechanization were coal-cutting, or punching, machines that were powered by compressed air. Soon thereafter the first application of electric engines was made, and compressed air gradually was replaced by electricity as the prime source of power. By the 1920s most mines were electrified, and the replacement of men and animals by machines began. It started to take fewer miners to produce more coal.

In the 1930s hydraulically controlled machines made mining even more of an automated industry. Continuous miners now cut and load coal in a single uninterrupted process, producing coal at a rapid rate with the use of a few skilled operators. Continuous belts are used to haul coal from the working face to the mine entrance or bottom of the shaft. The profile of the miner has necessarily changed with the times. Highly skilled men and women are required to operate the complicated mining machinery of today. The pick and shovel mining days are gone forever.

Early mining machinery.

1892 electric cutting machine.

Sullivan electric chain coal cutter.

Harrison pick machine.

No. 1 Works, Headframe at Grapevine Creek, McDowell County, 1903. *SWV*

Shaft and coal bin at No. 1 Works, 1904. *SWV*

A very old track-mounted cutting machine. Notice the enormous teeth. *WVU*

An early mining machine. *WVU*

An electric coal shuttle car. *WVU*

Operating a mining machine in Taylor County. *WVU*

A 1947 view of a loading machine in use. Machines such as this increased coal production and reduced the need for miners. *WVU*

Until the use of roof bolts came into use, mine timbers were used to hold up mine roofs. Thousands of different-sized timbers had to be hauled into the mines; sawmills were kept busy producing them. *WVU*

Miners going to work in an electric mine car into the main portal of the Pardee and Curtin No. 3 Mine, Bergoo, Webster County, 1930s. *WVU*

Miners unloading steel coal cars at Ream, McDowell County, 1938. *SWV*

An electric mine locomotive at Alpheus, McDowell County, 1922. *SWV*

ELECTRIC MINE MOTOR
1902.
Note-This motor still in use at #2 Mine. in 1922.

Miners riding in wooden coal cars. *WVU*

Underground ambulance used for transporting injured to the outside at the Hanna Company's Dunglen Mine No. 11. *WVU*

An underground mine pump used to pump water out of a mine, 1930. Water was a problem in the mines and had to be dealt with constantly to prevent flooding. *SWV*

A tandem twenty-six-ton Jeffery electric locomotive, Alpheus, McDowell County, 1930. *SWV*

Safety techniques also have seen great improvement over the years. In the old days mine gases and coal dust posed a dangerous problem; these hazards have now been reduced. Deep mines must be ventilated or continually flushed with fresh air to alleviate the danger of suffocation, poisoning, or explosion that can occur as a result of the buildup of mine gases, or "damp," such as methane (swamp gas), carbon dioxide, and carbon monoxide. Ventilation is accomplished by means of large, powerful fans that extract the mine air, thereby drawing fresh air into the mine through other portals or mine entrances.

Rock dusting is a technique used to allay the explosive potential of coal dust. Fine limestone dust, which is non-combustible, is spread on the coal. It combines with water that is present naturally and forms a protective coating. Limestone dust is also suspended in the air; when it mixes with the suspended coal dust it renders the latter nonexplosive.

Numerous other safety features have been developed since mining's early days. At first the roof over a coal seam was supported by timbers or pillars; now, however, roof bolts are used. These are large steel bolts several feet in length that are screwed into the roof rock, usually vertically, where they serve the same purpose as mine timbers.

The canary, highly sensitive to the presence of gas, was the miner's gas-detection tool in the early days. Today's safety inspectors constantly check for methane gas by using a methanometer capable of detecting a 0.1 percent gas concentration. *National Coal Association*

Testing for gas with safety lanterns was an intermediate step between the canary and the methanometer. *WVU*

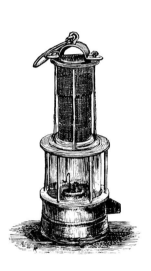

Various types of safety lanterns used mainly for gas detection.

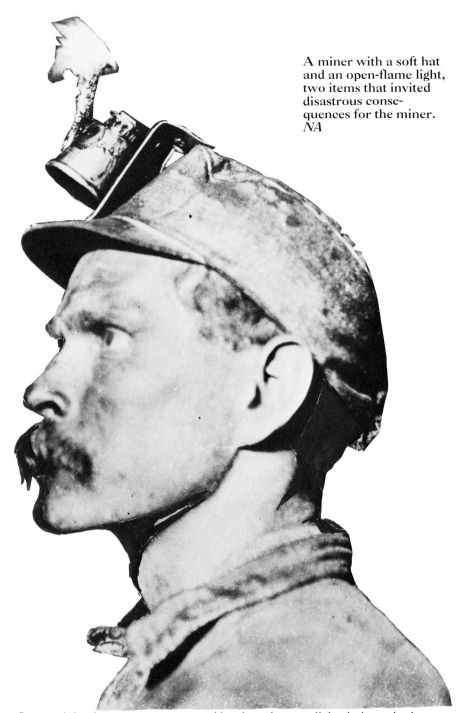

A miner with a soft hat and an open-flame light, two items that invited disastrous consequences for the miner. *NA*

Open-flame mining lamps were once used by the miners to light their work place, a dangerous practice. In the 1850s "lard oil" lamps were introduced. A small conical font held the lamp's fuel. There was a hinged snap cap to seal the top and a hook to attach the lamp to the miner's cap. A long spout extended outward from the font. The fuel was a mixture of lard and oil (cottonseed oil, kerosene, or crude oil) and gave off a choking, colored smoke. Later "sunshine" fuel, a mixture of paraffin wax and 3 percent mineral oil, which burned without smoking, was used.

The British invented a safety lamp in the late 1800s that had a wire-gauze screen around the flame to cool it. If any flame passed through the screen, it was too cool to ignite the methane. Its drawback was that it did not give off as much light as other lamps.

Also in the late 1800s the carbide lamp, which used a mixture of carbide and water, came into widespread use. It produced a good light but unfortunately retained the dangerous open flame. Battery-operated electric lights were developed later that did away with the open flames. They are still in use today.

THE CARBIDE LAMP

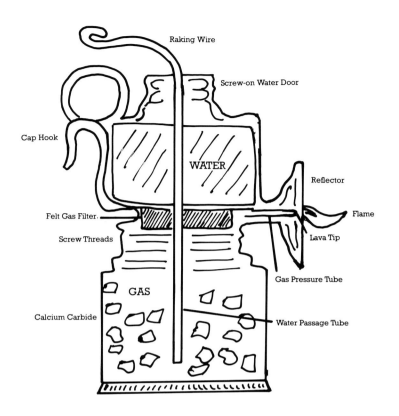

This popular mine lamp was developed in the late 1800s. When the enclosed carbide and water was mixed it produced a pungent gas-acetylene which burned with a bright yellow-white flame. The lamp burned for about four hours and gave good light but was dangerous with the open flame. The lamp contained an upper chamber for water and a lower one for carbide. A drip valve fed water to the lower chamber. Gas rose to the top, filtered through a felt pad and burned at the tip of a short spout. The flame could be adjusted from one to three inches. A safe battery-operated headlamp was eventually developed which is still in use today.

TIPPLES

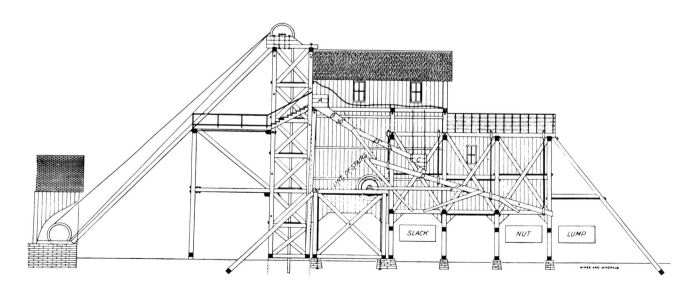

1903 drawing of a mine tipple. Screens separated the coal into "lump," "nut" and "slack" sizes.

Tipples were aptly named, for they were the buildings into which the coal cars were tipped when they came from the mines. Today's tipples provide crushing, washing, and sizing facilities for coal preparation.
National Coal Association

An early view of a coal-loading facility and powerhouse at the Cranberry Fuel Company, Raleigh County. *Author's collection*

An early coal-loading facility. *Author's collection*

Tipple at Kaymoor Mine No. 2, Fayette County, 1920. The south side piers for the New River Gorge bridge were placed on this site. *NPS*

An example of a coal-haulage system on a steep mountain gradient. Kaymoor Mine No. 1, Fayette County, 1920. *NPS*

A typical hillside tipple. *National Coal Association*

One system for hauling coal in the steep mountainous terrain was by aerial tramway. Cables that carried large buckets filled with coal to the tipples for processing and shipment were strung from ridge to ridge. This tramway was installed at Coalwood, McDowell County. The bucket is dropping slag on a slag pile. Circa 1924.   *SWV*

Skip hoist and tipple, Caretta, McDowell County, 1926.   *SWV*

Car loading at Mine 261, Caretta, 1926.   *SWV*

A coal-conveyor crossing the Tug River from Kentucky to a tipple on the West Virginia side (right) to the Portland Coal Company.   *SWV*

Safety became more of a concern in mining operations as mines expanded and went deeper into the mountains. This accident board was erected at the Gary, McDowell County operations of U.S. Steel in the 1920s.   *SWV*

A coal-washing plant in 1962 along Beaver Creek and State Route 3, Nicholas County.   *U.S. Forest Service*

Installing a huge Jeffery fan for air circulation at the Coalwood mine, McDowell County, 1920s. *SWV*

A large fan at U.S. Steel's Mine No. 4, Thorpe, McDowell County, in 1905. It was important to provide proper ventilation in the mines to reduce the danger of gas accumulation and explosion. *SWV*

A picking table with newly installed Mercury vapor lights. Slate and other noncoal pieces were pulled off the belt by these pickers. *WVU*

Interior view of the tipple at Caretta, McDowell County, 1926. *SWV*

Rotary dump in a tipple at the Lamar Collieries, Lamar, Mercer County. *WVU*

Locker rooms were provided for the miners by the larger companies. Notice how the miners' clothes were put in baskets or hung by chains from the ceiling. Top: Industrial Collieries, Barrackville No. 41 Mine, Marion County, 1946. Bottom: Typical Consolidated Coal Company locker room. *LC; WVU*

At large mining operations, modern showers were provided to allow the miners to clean up after a day's work. *WVU*

Typical barracks for miners in the late 1880s. Conditions were austere for these men who usually worked ten to twelve hours a day, six days a week. *WVU*

Going to work on foot with their lunch pails, Grafton, Taylor County. *WVU*

An all-too-familiar sight in many coal mines through the years. *WVU*

Areas worked by giant coal cutters leave unusual designs in the coal seams. *WVU*

Waiting to go to work. Maps on the wall show the extent of the underground mining operations. *WVU*

To make a good day's wage, this sign was strictly adhered to. *WVU*

Strip mining is a more recent development in the wresting of coal from the mountains. It had to wait for the development of large steam shovels to strip away the overburden. This strip operation was located near Hardesty, Marion County, in 1925. *WVU*

A 1944 view of miners boring holes for blasting powder using compressed air drills. *WVU*

The Norfolk and Western Railway produced a movie showing mining operations in a mine three hundred feet deep. This is believed to be the first use of color film inside a mine. It was probably filmed during the post-World War II era. *WVU*

Vital to winning World War II was production on the home front. Coal was an important mineral necessary to power the nation's factories, and a steady flow was essential to the war effort. Miners coming off shift from No. 34 Mine, Bishop, McDowell County, 1943. *WVU*

Before World War II it was almost impossible for a man past forty-five to find a job in the mines. With the war taking the younger men, however, older retired miners were called back to work. In a northern mine, John Prunty (right), age seventy-two, watches blacksmith Henry Saunders (left), age seventy. Both men had worked in the mines for nearly sixty years, and each was once a mine foreman. *AP/Wide World Photos, Inc.*

COAL BARONS

Like its counterpart in the West, coal mining in West Virginia spawned its share of men who built and developed the industry: the coal barons. The rapid expansion of mining in the state following the Civil War could not have happened without a large influx of out-of-state capital, not only to open and operate the mines themselves but also to develop the railroads necessary to haul the coal through the rugged mountainous terrain. A special group of financiers that was not afraid to gamble to build its empires was needed.

Many of the early entrepreneurs came from out of state; some went on to fame and fortune in business and politics. A notable example of one of West Virginia's coal barons was Henry Gassaway Davis. Davis got his start working as a brakeman for the Baltimore and Ohio Railroad and by 1847 was supervisor of the line to Cumberland. He later was able to acquire rich coal and timber lands in the state and organized the West Virginia Central and Pittsburgh Railroad and the Coal and Coke Railroad to develop his holdings. Several towns in the northern coalfields were established as a result of his railroads.

Davis served in the West Virginia legislature and in 1870 was elected to the first of his two terms in the U.S. Senate. He became the "grand old man" of West Virginia politics and in 1904 was the Democratic party's unsuccessful nominee for vice-president of the United States. Davis died at the age of ninety-one.

There were numerous others who rose to prominence through their activities in the coal industry in the state, among them William McKell, Jenkin Jones, W.D. Thurmond, and Joseph L. Beury, who shipped the first coal out of the New River fields. The era of the coal barons is long over, however. Giant coal companies, many of which are subsidiaries of even larger oil companies, now control the bulk of the state's coal industry.

WILLIAM HENRY EDWARDS—born in 1822 in New York. He became interested in surveying coal in the Kanawha Valley and acquired thousands of acres of coal lands along Paint Creek in the late 1840s. He settled in Coalburg and opened his first mine in 1853, later becoming the president of the Ohio and Kanawha Coal Company. Edwards was also interested in scientific and literary pursuits. *SWV*

JUSTUS COLLINS—born in Alabama. Collins moved to Goodwill in Mercer County in 1887 to establish the Louisville Coal & Coke Company. He opened numerous mines in the area and in 1929 formed the Winding Gulf Collieries. Collins recruited miners from all over the country to work in his mines and was a prominent figure in the southern coalfields until his death in 1934. *SWV*

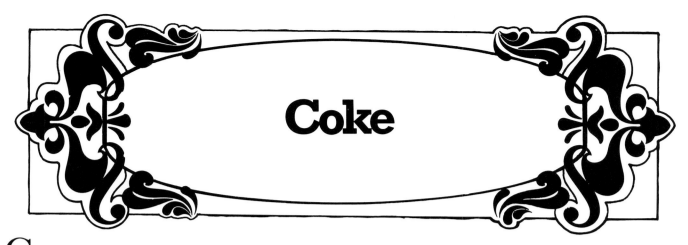

Coke

COKE, ONCE the most important by-product of coal, is derived by burning the volatile matter (i.e., the tars, oils, and gases) from the coal, leaving only fixed carbon. This is accomplished by the process of halting the combustion before it is allowed to burn the carbon.

The origins of this substance date back to the dawning of the Iron Age, when it was discovered that it would take the oxygen out of iron ore when burned, and convert the ore to metal. For centuries charcoal was used for this purpose, but by the early 1700s a shortage of wood in the industrial nations prompted a search for a suitable substitute. An Englishman is credited with being the first to successfully produce coke from coal, in approximately 1711, and in Europe coke quickly took over the role that had been played by charcoal.

The iron-making industry in America continued to use charcoal until that nation's wood shortage in the 1830s. Anthracite or hard coal, which was found in large quantities in eastern Pennsylvania close to the major iron-making sites, was gradually substituted for charcoal. It was not until the late 1800s, however, with the increased demand for railroad iron following the Civil War, the adoption of the Bessemer process in steel making, and the availability of low-priced, high-quality coking coal, that coke became the primary fuel for iron and steel production. By the end of World War I, 88 percent of the nation's iron and steel was produced by the process of using coke.

Largely because of its vast quantities of coking coal, the United States soon became the major producer of iron and steel in the world. A great percentage of this coking coal was found in West Virginia, and numerous coke plants were built along the railroad lines. Most of these plants used "beehive" ovens (dome-shaped ovens, shaped like old-

Workers erecting beehive ovens at the Louisville Coal & Coke Company in Goodwill, Mercer County, in the 1880s. *WVU*

style beehives) to produce coke. During the 1920s, however, beehive ovens were replaced by the more efficient by-product ovens, which could recover the gas and other valuable chemicals lost in the earlier process.

Coke ovens continued to operate throughout the coal regions of the state into the late 1970s. Now, however, they no longer burn; they have become a thing of the past.

Coke ovens in production along the Chesapeake and Ohio Railway on the New River in 1897. *NPS*

A good example of operating coke ovens in the state around 1910. A tremendous amount of smoke was released into the atmosphere by the ovens. *WVU*

Views of the construction of beehive ovens at Gary, McDowell County. Top: Band ovens of the No. 2 works, looking south, 1903. Bottom: Skilled craftsmen, many of whom were new immigrants from Italy and southern Europe, were required to build these brick and stone structures. *SWV*

No.6 Works Bank Ovens looking N'ly towards Coal Bin. November 8, 1903.

Building coke ovens in the early 1900s. A tremendous amount of brick and stone work was required. *WVU*

As noted, coke ovens produced heavy, impenetrable smoke over a large area, day and night. These operated at Longacre, Fayette County, in 1938. *LC*

Coke ovens at Smithers, Fayette County. Ovens in this area were in operation into the late 1940s.   *SWV*

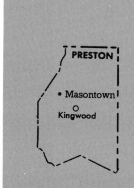

ELKINS COAL & COKE COMPANY

A prime example of a large beehive coke-oven complex is still in existence in Preston County. The old Elkins Coal & Coke Company operation, now listed on the National Register of Historic Places, is located one-half mile southwest of Masontown and one-fourth mile west of West Virginia Route 7, near the small community of Bretz. The complex, which covers thirty-six acres, consists of the remains of 140 beehive coke ovens, ruins of the original buildings, and several pieces of vintage equipment. The remains date from the heyday of the company's production, 1906 until 1919.

Stephen B. Elkins, a prominent West Virginia coal and railroad operator, acquired large coal tracts in the area in the 1890s. In 1902 he purchased the uncompleted Morgantown and Kingwood Railroad in order to fully exploit his coalfields. His company acquired the town of Bretz and an adjacent coal mine in 1906 and began the construction of a bank of four hundred ovens. The ovens were put into full production in 1907, following the completion of the route connecting Elkins' railroad with the Baltimore and Ohio. This route gave the company an eastward connection to its chief customer, the huge steel plant and shipyard at Sparrow's Point, Maryland.

Bethlehem Steel Company purchased the Bretz operation from Elkins and in 1920 shut down the ovens. The property subsequently passed through a number of hands, with the ovens operating only intermittently during periods of peak steel production. A new company took over the operation in 1953 and produced coke there until well in the 1970s. All the ovens now lie dormant, producing nothing but memories of the days of coke production in the state.

The ovens looking east.

West-facing ovens.

View to the west of the operation.

An old coal car that once fed coal into the tops of the ovens. These cars were called Larrys, possibly after the British word for truck, Lorry.

An old coke-loading machine.

Shop building.

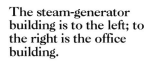

The steam-generator building is to the left; to the right is the office building.

Many of the ovens are now caved in.

Many of the ovens are now caved in.

Some of the original ovens, however, still remain in good condition.

The opening in the top of one of the ovens, into which the coal was fed.

Company Stores and Towns

Most of the coal towns that emerged with the opening of the coalfields in the 1880s were located in relatively isolated areas of the state. Accessibility to food, clothing, and other goods the miners and their families needed for day-to-day living was therefore a problem. To supply these necessities, the larger coal companies established company stores. Although most coal companies were in the retail business from necessity instead of choice, many of these stores did help the profit structures of their companies, especially during the depression years.

Company stores provided practically everything the mining family needed for its daily existence. For many years, the company stores had a virtual monopoly on the miner's business, for other concerns could not compete in such isolated surroundings. Retailers from the larger towns such as Charleston, Beckley, and Bluefield would send trucks selling clothing, household items, and the like into the coalfields. The miners could also order from the various mail-order catalogs of the day. The majority of business transactions, however, took place in the company stores.

A common misconception concerning company stores is that all of the coal companies used their stores as a hold over the miners, forcing them to buy all their goods at the stores or risk losing their jobs. It is unfortunate that this was the case in some instances; generally, however, the stores were there only to provide a service to the isolated community.

The company store was usually the focal point for each small mining community. Miners were often given credit at the stores in the form of scrip, which could be traded for food, clothing, and other goods. All the necessities of living were provided for the workers by the company in one location. This Consolidated Coal Company store was located at Owings, in Marion County, near Fairmont. *SWV Consolidation Collection*

Company stores were stark and drab by today's standards, but they offered the basic necessities and at times even some frills. They often housed the post office and were the centers of community activities.

Company store, Montana Mines. *WVU*

Company store, Chiefton. *WVU*

Company store, Bellview Mine, Marion County. *WVU*

Caretta, McDowell County, company store, 1923. *SWV*

The Pocahontas Collieries Company store at Premier, McDowell County. *WVU*

The store and saloon of the Superior Pocahontas Coal Company at Davy, McDowell County. Notice the saloon has BEER ON ICE. *WVU*

The store and office at
Beury, Fayette
County. *WVU*

An old company store
near Oak Hill, Fayette
County. *Daniel E.
Davidson, Charleston*

This magnificent stone
building of the Island
Creek Coal Company
in Holden, Logan
County, on Route 119, is
still in existence. *WVU*

SCRIP

As previously noted, in the early years most coal mines in the state were located in remote areas, away from the centers of commerce. U.S. currency, therefore, was difficult to keep on hand, and many companies chose instead to issue scrip tokens as payment for wages. It is conjectured that the first scrip issuer in West Virginia was the Pioneer Coal Company, incorporated in 1855 at Campbell's Creek near Charleston. The use of scrip rapidly spread to other industries throughout the country, and tokens dated as early as the 1880s and 1890s have been found by collectors. Scrip continued to be used into the 1950s.

Scrip tokens could be exchanged at the company stores for food, clothing, household supplies, and the like. Payment by scrip served a dual purpose. The miner could get wages in advance of his regular paycheck, and he did not have to borrow money or charge items at the store. The company in turn did not need to keep extensive charge account records, nor were there difficult collection problems involved.

It was easy to identify the scrip issued by an individual company, for each company designed its tokens to be unique by virtue of size, shape, or brand. A few companies dated their scrip, but it was more common to change the tokens' size, shape, or brand at certain intervals. This allowed the company to reissue its scrip occasionally and also discouraged counterfeiting.

The first scrip was in paper coupon form, hence the name. It began to be issued in metal form about 1920, most frequently in brass but also in copper and aluminum. During World War II, the tokens were produced in a fiber material in order to save metal for the war effort. The most common denominations were 25¢, 50¢ and $1.00.

As with any system of this sort, certain abuses arose. Some companies paid their miners in scrip alone, forcing them to shop exclusively in the company store, where the goods were usually higher priced. In addition, many miners habitually drew their wages in scrip in advance of payday. Their tokens were then cashed at a discount of as much as 50 percent and the money spent for items that were not necessities. As a result of these abuses, some states outlawed the use of scrip. Economic conditions dictated the use of scrip to a large degree.

Fayetteville boasts the headquarters of the National Scrip Collectors Association, which has over six hundred members at present. With industries in thirty-two states once issuing scrip and more than ten thousand varieties of coal scrip alone, its availability has turned scrip collecting into an increasingly popular hobby.

Tokens courtesy Walter Caldwell, Fayetteville

NAMING THE TOWNS*

Scanning a map of West Virginia, especially the coalfield areas, one is struck by the unusual names of many of the towns. Some have simply disappeared under the changing coal economy, but many linger on, mostly in name only.

Coal-town names stand out because they fail to conform to the expected rules of nomenclature; the larger and older cities and towns of the state generally followed these rules, being named for famous people, early settlers, or landmarks found in the area. Since coal towns were often established literally overnight for the one purpose of mining the area's black gold, the names did not have time to evolve organically over generations of popular usage. Rather they were assigned abruptly by the men and companies that built the towns.

The reasoning behind coal-town names runs the gamut from the inspired to the ridiculous. Coal men were often colorful individuals and, as a result, frequently gave colorful names to their towns. Many towns were named after the coal operators themselves; hence names such as Eccles, Page, and Tams are still on the map. Several names were derived from a combination of the operator's first and last names or initials, such as Itmann for I.T. Mann or Jenkinjones for Jenkin Jones.

Other towns received names in honor of a prominent person in the coal industry. Iaeger, for large landowner Colonel William Iaeger, and Gary, for Judge Elbert Gary, the president of U.S. Steel who established several towns to provide coal for his large steel mills, are examples of these.

Women were not left out, either. Glen Jean was named for operator T.G. McKell's wife, Jean Dun, and other towns, some gone and forgotten, were named for wives, mothers, and even sweethearts. Acronyms were also common. Some of these included Besoco for the Beckley Smokeless Coal Company, Ameagle for the American Eagle Colliery, and Grayeagle for the Gray Eagle Coal Company.

There was no end to the name game. Matoaka and Iroquois were named for Indian tribes, Hiawatha for Longfellow's hero. Scarbro and Carlisle were named after English towns, and Kopperston's namesake was its creator, the great Koppers Company. As many of the pioneer operators were of British origin, they originated the custom of prefixing the British "glen" to town names. Thus we have Glen Jean, Glen Rogers, and Glen Alum.

Coal baron Sam Dixon was forced to change the names of two of his towns following explosions at their mines in 1906 and 1907. Parral and Stuart became Summerlee and Lochgelly, respectively, in an attempt to overcome the adverse publicity that made it difficult to employ miners following the disasters.

The United States Post Office finally had to step in and try to control the naming of towns. There were so many small towns with the same or similar names that the resulting confusion was great. One of the great legacies of the colorful bygone era of coal mining lies in the names of its towns. Where else could one find a town such as that of Cinco in Kanawha County? Cinco, by the way, was named for the founder's favorite brand of cigars.

---

*Portions of this chapter were taken from *Goldenseal* magazine's editor Ken Sullivan's article "Naming the Coal Towns," published in the January-March 1978 issue.

Pentress

Eccles

Isaban

Wolf Pen

WAR

TAMS

BERGOO

MASONTOWN

Idamay

Glen Jean

This well-planned community is Kempton, Preston County. Many of the coal towns built to house miners were well designed, especially if the town was located in an area of large coal deposits and would be in existence for many years, circa 1930s. *LC*

Matoaka

Kermit

ALUM CREEK

Wyatt

JERE

RAMAGE

IAEGER

Newburg

Miners' houses at
Wyatt, Harrison Coun-
ty, 1909.   *WVU*

A black camp at Hemp-
hill, McDowell County.
NA

Beury, Fayette County,
along the New River in
1915.   *NPS*

The house of coal
baron J.L. Beury in the
town with his name,
Beury, Fayette County.
WVU

Coalwood, McDowell
County, and the Carter
Coal Company, July
1937. *Norfolk & West-
ern Railway*

Barrackville, Marion
County, a mining town
in the northern coal-
fields, circa 1920s.
SWV

Boarded-up homes in
the abandoned mining
town of Twin Branch,
McDowell County, in
1938. The town was
once owned by Henry
Ford. He closed it
down, rather than
letting in the union.
LC

Primitive miners' cabins
at Osage, Monongalia
County, in 1946. It
would take many years
for conditions such as
these to improve.   *NA*

The Wyatt Coal Com-
pany town of Sharon,
Kanawha County, in
1946.   *NA*

A typical southern coal mining community near Welch, McDowell County. This photo is one of a series taken by Marion Post Wolcott for the Farm Security Administration in 1938. *LC*

Bluefield, Mercer County, in 1946. The city was and still is a major rail center for the shipment of coal east and west. *NA*

The Anawalt post office in the center of the McDowell coalfields. *SWV*

Two views of Gary, McDowell County. The town was named in 1896 for Elbert Gary, an official of the U.S. Steel Corporation. In 1902 the company completed one of the world's largest coal-processing plants here. Top: Typical miners' houses. Bottom: Constructing the Gary National Bank. *SWV*

Weirton Coal Company's Isabella Mine, Northern Panhandle, circa 1940s.   *WVU*

Another important coal town is Williamson, Mingo County. This was a July 4th celebration in 1921 in front of the courthouse.   *WVU*

Main street of Davy, McDowell County, in 1938. This photo is a good example of the importance of the railroad to the mining community. These are tracks of the Norfolk and Western Railway. *LC*

Street scene, Logan, Logan County, in the 1920s. Logan is in the heart of the southern coalfields. *WVU*

Slab Fork Coal Company and the town of Slab Fork, Raleigh County, in 1947. *Author's collection*

Main street of Welch, McDowell County, in the southern coalfields, 1942.   *NA*

Part of the town of Williamson, Mingo County, 1935. Notice the small shacks built around the coal facilities. Crops would be planted on any level piece of ground, especially during these depression years.   *LC*

Welch, McDowell County, along the Tug Fork River in 1938.   *LC*

MacDonald, Fayette County, and the MacDonald Coal Company. *Author's collection*

Main street of Mt. Hope, circa 1920s. Mt. Hope is one of several Fayette County towns dependent on the coal industry for a major part of its business life. *Author's collection*

Gulf Smokeless Coal Company, Tams, Raleigh County. This town, which is still in existence, was founded by W.P. Tams, Jr., in 1909. *Author's collection*

The largest remaining building in Tams, Raleigh County.

THURMOND

Southern West Virginia was finally linked to the East Coast at Tidewater, Virginia, on January 29, 1873, with the driving of the golden spike on the Chesapeake and Ohio Railway. The completion of the Chesapeake and Ohio opened up the New River coalfields, and the town of Thurmond in Fayette County was born.

Thurmond, named for Captain W.P. Thurmond of the Confederate Army, was to become one of the most important freight stations in the eastern United States. In 1910 alone, the station handled over four million tons of freight with a worth of almost five million dollars. That same year, over seventy-six thousand passengers used the station facility. These figures were far greater than those for the larger cities of the East and West.

Thurmond was indeed unique. For years it was the only town in the world without a street; there was not a single road leading in or out of town. Thurmond's main thoroughfare was the tracks of the Chesapeake and Ohio. Even though its population never exceeded five hundred, the town boasted two banks. There was but one store; it did a booming $6000 per month business and never took in a dollar in U.S. currency. All sales were transacted using scrip.

The social activities of Thurmond centered around the town's famous Dunglen Hotel, built in 1901 by William McKell, one of the area's coal barons. The Dunglen had one hundred rooms, and, according to legend, its bar never closed and its gambling rooms did not cease operation from the day the hotel opened until the state's prohibition legislation went into effect in 1914. The longest poker game in history, rumored to have lasted 14 years, is said to have taken place at the Dunglen.

The following story is illustrative of the early, violent days of Thurmond. It was recorded by a former superintendent of one of the area's mines:

> Someone discovered the body of a drowned man floating in New River one morning not far from the famous Dunglen. This was nothing new, strange or startling in the period of time. The Mayor and ex-officio Coroner was sent for and the body was removed from the river. The pockets of the deceased were searched and a pistol and $25 in cash were found. The Mayor immediately fined the victim the $25 for carrying a gun—took the gun and cash—and notified the county officials to bury the man, which the county did at a cost of $10 to the taxpayer.

Aerial view

By 1930 Thurmond had lost its prominence as a business center. The Dunglen burned down that year and most commercial activity in the region shifted to other towns that were connected by highways. Worked-out coal mines and the depression years eventually turned most of the New River Canyon towns into ghost towns.

There has recently been a revival of interest in Thurmond. The town has been listed on the National Register of Historic Places, and the National Park Service has designated the New River Canyon a national recreation area. Whitewater rafting companies now use the area extensively, and tourism is increasing. The future is looking brighter for the town that made *Ripley's Believe It or Not* three times during its heyday.

Opposite: The famous Dunglen Hotel in Thurmond, Fayette County. It was constructed in 1901 and burned down in 1930. *Author's collection*

Present-day scenes of
Thurmond. *NPS*

Railroad building in
foreground and the re-
mains of the once-flour-
ishing town.

Main line of the Chesa-
peake & Ohio Railway.

Remaining buildings
along the railroad
tracks. On the left is the
Bankers Club, now
operating as a cafe, and
on the right is the old
Mankin Drug Com-
pany.

Bramwell, in the western area of Mercer County, in the late 1920s. This was at one time the richest coal town in West Virginia, and many coal barons' houses are still standing.   *WVU*

One of the impressive homes still standing in the town. This was the home of I.T. Mann, president of the Bramwell Bank.

Scenes in present-day Bramwell

The famous Bramwell bank, at one time reported to be the richest small bank in the United States. It was established in 1889 and became the largest bank in deposits in the state before closing in 1933.

Main street of Bramwell.

One of the impressive homes still standing in the town. This was the home of well-known coal baron Philip Goodwill.

In a scene reminiscent of many Western ghost towns (except for the lush vegetation) sits the town of Giatto in Mercer County. One can almost visualize the train puffing down the main street with kids and dogs running after it. *SWV*

GHOST TOWNS

When one hears the term ghost town, what usually comes to mind is the western scene of sagebrush blowing down an abandoned street of deserted, broken-down buildings. West Virginia, however, has its share of these towns, for coal mining is in that respect no different than hard rock mining that was done in the West. Both types of mines were either worked out through the years or fell victim to the economics of the time.

Many of the western ghost towns seem destined to remain as they are for years to come; those in the eastern part of the country usually meet a different fate. The weather conditions and vegetation growth in the East reclaim an area sooner. Also, because of the more confined spaces and larger populations of the East, the eastern ghost towns are more likely to be resettled for other purposes or simply plowed under or strip mined away.

The largest concentrations of ghost towns remaining in West Virginia are found in the remote regions of the New River coalfields. There the remains of tipples, company stores, and houses can be found. There are also several towns and many structures left in other parts of the state. Let us hope that a few of these sites survive to serve as a reminder of the early days of coal mining in West Virginia.

The bank at Glen Jean, a boom town from the late 1880s until the Great Depression. The bank, one of Fayette County's most celebrated architectural landmarks, was constructed in 1909 and served as the hub of the financial empire started by Thomas McKell in 1873 and continued by his son, William. The McKells owned vast interests in coal properties, railroads and land. The building is now registered on the National Register of Historical Places.

Unions and Strife in the Coalfields

THE HISTORY of the mine wars and union strife in West Virginia is reminiscent of the warfare in Europe prior to and during World War I. For years the state was an armed camp, with insurrection and rebellion in the coalfields. The struggle of miner against coal operator could be called West Virginia's second Civil War. It eventually involved county and state politicians, the U.S. Army, and even the President of the United States.

Only the highlights of this period in the state's history can be included in a book of this scope. Many books are available on the subject if a more detailed study is desired; Howard Lee's *Bloodletting in Appalachia*, for example, contains a vivid portrayal of these bloody days.

During the main period of conflict, from 1912 until 1921, labor violence erupted throughout the state. Political corruption was rampant, from the local level all the way to the heads of the state legislature. There was at one point even a threat to take over the capitol in Charleston. The justice system in the state was stretched beyond its capacity to serve its citizens. Several other states also had their share of labor troubles. It was perhaps the darkest period of labor confrontation in American history.

The vast coalfields of the state were opened to major exploitation by the expansion of the railroads in the late 1800s. The entrepreneurs who took advantage of this new accessibility were for the most part a hardy breed and fiercely independent. Many became large operators, "coal barons," and their power and influence was widespread.

The miners, however, did not share in the operators' newfound wealth. Thousands of workers and their families had poured into the state, mainly from Europe and the South, with the opening of the coalfields. They often were forced to live in company

Union miners being evicted from their homes at the Liberty Fuel Company mine in 1924. This was a common occurrence in the coalfields during the days of union strife. Since the coal companies usually owned the miners' houses, this was one way the operators could get back at the miners when they went on strike. *WVU*

towns, usually in substandard housing, and at times to buy only from the company stores. There were great inequities in the way the miners were treated and paid. It was only natural that under these conditions conflict would arise between the miners and the mine operators.

To protect their holdings, the operators hired mine guards, frequently from the Baldwin-Felts Detective Agency in Bluefield. These guards were employed supposedly to maintain law and order in the camps; the law of the camps, however, was at times in direct conflict with the established law enforcement in the counties. In reality the guards were there to keep the miners from joining the union or causing trouble in the camps.

If a miner was considered an agitator, showing an interest in the union, he was usually fired and blacklisted in all the other mining camps in the area. One method of keeping the union out of the coalfields was to compel miners to sign a document known as a yellow-dog contract before going to work. This simply stated that the prospective worker was not a member of nor would become a member of the United Mine Workers of America (UMWA) as shown below:

CONTRACT OF EMPLOYMENT

I am employed by and work for the _____ Company, of _____, West Virginia, with the express understanding that I am not a member of the United Mine Workers of America, and will not become so while an employee of said _____ Company; that said Company agrees to run an "Open Shop" while I am employed by said _____ Company. If at any time I want to join or become connected with the United Mine Workers of America, or any affiliated organization, I agree to withdraw from the employment of said Company, and I further agree that while I am in the employ of said Company that I will not make any efforts amongst its employees to bring about the unionization of said employees against the Company's wishes. I have either read the above or it has been read to me.

Dated this the _____day of _____, 19____.

(Signed)_____

The struggle to unionize all the mines in West Virginia would continue until 1933, when Franklin D. Roosevelt's New Deal legislation forced the coal operators to allow the union into the mines. For over three decades, the conflict between labor and management was waged in the state, with hundreds of men killed, thousands evicted from their homes, and coal production halted for months as a result.

It is a sad chapter in the state's history.

Thomas L. Felts, co-owner with William G. Baldwin of the Baldwin-Felts Detective Agency, headquartered in Bluefield. *SWV*

BALDWIN-FELTS AGENCY

Mine guards were a phenomenon in labor history peculiar to the first part of the twentieth century. These were men ostensibly hired by the coal companies to provide security and maintain law and order at the mines. In reality, they spent most of their time keeping union activity out of the mines and seeing that the miners observed company policy.

The most influential and largest of the agencies specializing in supplying mine guards to both the southern and northern coalfields was the Baldwin-Felts Detective Agency, headquartered in Bluefield. The agency was founded in the early 1900s by William G. Baldwin and Thomas L. Felts and became one of the largest such agencies in the United States. Their employees virtually ruled the coalfields into the early 1900s, primarily by physical threats and the barrel of a gun. During the large mine wars, the agency would hire literally hundreds of guards to battle the miners. In several counties, agency men were appointed deputy sheriffs, in direct conflict with state law.

Following federal legislation allowing unionization in 1933, the Baldwin-Felts Agency went out of business, its services no longer needed.

The mine guard system was not completely abolished until the administration of Governor Homer Holt in 1937.

A group of Baldwin-Felts detectives decked out in their finest attire in 1901. *NPS*

This Baldwin-Felts mine guard looks as if he means business. His outfit is impressive, perhaps worn to intimidate the miners. *Author's collection*

UNITED MINE WORKERS OF AMERICA

The United Mine Workers of America (UMWA) was formed on January 25, 1890, by the merger of two rival coal miners' unions that had been competing for ascendency for fifty years. The need for one strong union to represent the miners in the coalfields was tremendous. Miners worked long hours in hazardous, back-breaking conditions, often beginning as young children. John Mitchell, the first UMWA president, worked to abolish child labor and establish the eight-hour workday.

John L. Lewis, the union's legendary leader, became its president in 1920 and ruled with an iron hand for the next forty years. During this time, the union achieved a guaranteed eight-hour day, national wage agreements, and much-needed safety legislation.

The fight to organize the southern coalfields in West Virginia was a Herculean task. Violence against union supporters was common, with eviction of the miners from company-owned houses the order of the day for strikers and sympathizers.

The violence ended only with the passage in 1933 of the National Industrial Recovery Act, legislation that gave workers the right to join the labor organization of their choice. Miners joined the UMWA in record numbers, the membership increasing by three hundred thousand in only one year.

Fred Mooney, left, secretary-treasurer of District No. 17, and Frank Keeney, president of the district. These men were two of the leaders of the 1921 March on Logan. *SWV*

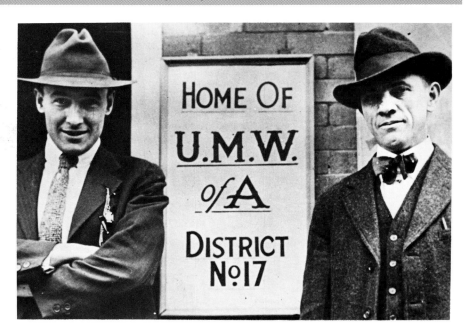

In 1946, Lewis defied a court injunction and led the UMWA in a major strike, causing President Truman to seize the mines. In the settlement, however, the miners won the establishment of the Welfare and Retirement Fund, which provided medical care, hospitalization, treatment for disabled workers, death benefits, and pensions for retired miners. This was one of Lewis' greatest achievements.

The 1950s saw the beginnings of the mechanization of the coal industry, a move that resulted in the lay-offs of many miners. Lewis supported mechanization on the theory that increased productivity would result in more resources for the Welfare and Retirement Fund. This was not the case, however; by 1960 only 170,000 miners were employed, as compared to 450,000 in 1947, and benefits were beginning to be cut.

W.A. "Tony" Boyle succeeded Lewis following his retirement but failed to attract the support from the membership that Lewis had known. Boyle was challenged for the presidency in 1969 by International Executive Board member Joseph "Jock" Yablonski. The election was initially won by Boyle, but the results were later overturned by a federal court and a second election ordered. Yablonski, along with his wife and daughter, was murdered before the new election, and Boyle was eventually convicted of having ordered the killings. He was subsequently sentenced to life in prison.

Arnold Miller, a native West Virginian, was elected the UMWA's new president. During his administration, which coincided with the coal boom of the seventies, the union won cost-of-living increases, more benefits, and the return of the coverage that had been cut from the Welfare and Retirement Fund. An increased emphasis on democratic reforms resulted in the establishment of the right of the rank and file to vote on their contracts. Safety measures were also toughened. Nineteen sixty-nine saw the passage of the Federal Coal Mine Health and Safety Act, and in 1974 the miners won the right to refuse unsafe work.

Miller was forced to retire due to ailing health in 1979, two years before his term was to expire. Sam Church finished the term but was defeated in 1982 by Richard L. Trumka. Trumka has worked since his election for relief programs for the unemployed, a reorganized safety and health program, and more involvement in organizing by the members.

The major problem facing the union today remains unemployment. Relaxed enforcement of health and safety standards is also an important concern.

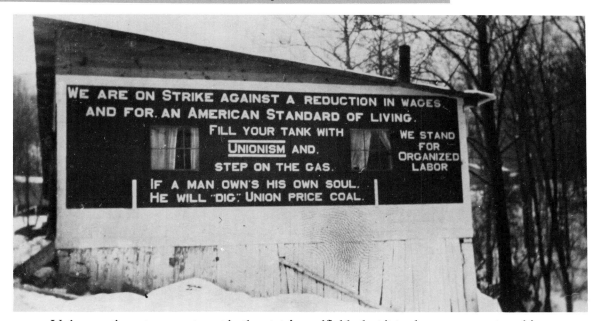

Union sentiments were strong in the state's coalfields, but it took many years to achieve almost complete unionization of the coal companies. *WVU*

Union banners in the collection of the Beckley Exhibition Coal Mine.

JOHN L. LEWIS

John Llewellyn Lewis, born in Lucas, Iowa, in 1880, was an important figure in West Virginia history and one of the most powerful labor leaders in America. He became acting president of the United Mine Workers of America in 1919 and was elected president the following year. He was to hold this post for the next forty years, until his retirement in 1960.

Lewis' career was marked by bitter strikes and sharp conflicts with union opponents. He challenged the craft organization of the American Federaton of Labor (AFL) by forming the Committee for Industrial Organization in 1935. Unions that joined the CIO were suspended by the AFL Executive Council in 1936 and ousted in 1938. In that year, the CIO formed its own federation and changed its name to the Congress of Industrial Organizations. Under Lewis' leadership, the CIO organized strong industrial unions in the mass-production industries.

Lewis took the UMWA out of the CIO in 1942. The union rejoined the AFL in 1946 but has been unaffiliated since 1947. With Lewis' death in 1969, an era in American labor history came to an end.

John L. Lewis as a young man. *WVU*

Lewis was a tough union president. *SWV*

PAINT CREEK AND CABIN CREEK

The thirty-year fight to unionize all of West Virginia's coal mines began along Paint and Cabin creeks, just south of the capital city of Charleston. In April 1912, seventy-five hundred miners at approximately one hundred different mines went on strike. Most of the Kanawha River coalfields were already unionized; for years, however, the operators along the two creeks had resisted the union.

The miners made several demands to the operators: (1) blacklisting was to be halted; (2) the miners were to be allowed to unionize; (3) cribbing was to be stopped; (4) scales were to be installed at each mine to give the miners an accurate tonnage weight; (5) compulsory trading at company stores was no longer to be allowed, and (6) docking penalties were to be determined by two check-weighmen, one of whom was to be employed by the miners.

All the demands were refused, and a bitter strike ensued. Baldwin-Felts detectives were hired by the operators to break the strike. Striking miners and their families were evicted from their company-owned homes, and scab (nonunion) labor was brought in to reopen the mines.

A U.S. Senate committee headed by Senator William Borah of Idaho investigated the strike, finding much evidence of abuse against the miners. The West Virginia Legislature also conducted an inquiry. No action was taken, however, and the coal operators set up pillboxes and fortifications in the fields in anticipation of armed conflict.

Governor Henry D. Hatfield settled the Paint Creek strike. *SWV*

At the height of the confrontation, eighty-two-year-old Mary Harris "Mother" Jones, a fiery union organizer, appeared on the scene. She gave a speech on the state capitol grounds, in which she advocated armed aggression by the miners to rid the creeks of the hated mine guards. Governor William Glasscock, whom Mother Jones violently denounced, tried to arbitrate a settlement, but both sides rejected his proposals.

Both the miners and the mine operators armed themselves for the inevitable confrontation. Several guards were killed, and small skirmishes occurred up and down the creeks. A larger battle took place at Mucklow, on Paint Creek, in which at least sixteen guards and miners were killed.

On September 1, 1912, union miners from the area joined the strikers; over six thousand armed men converged on Cabin Creek for a showdown. The days of 1861-65 appeared to be recurring the next day when Governor Glasscock declared the strike area under martial law and sent in twelve hundred militia. Both the guards and strikers were ordered to disarm, and military courts were established. The miners were prohibited from assembling in large numbers. Mother Jones reappeared, attempting to read the Declaration of Independence to a group of strikers. The old woman was arrested but soon released.

On October 15 martial law was lifted. Soon afterward, however, some of the soldiers joined forces with the mine guards, and early in November things heated up once more. Scab workers were fired upon, as were the trains transporting coal from the area, and the strikers soon had the upper hand. The governor reissued the martial law order on November 15. Military councils were reestablished and many strikers jailed. The second order came to an end on January 10, 1913, although nothing had been settled.

In February 1913, an armored train equipped with machine guns by the coal operators sped by the strikers' tent city and fired upon the inhabitants. One miner was killed, several wounded. Three days later the third martial law order was issued and military courts once again instituted. Mother Jones was again arrested and this time sentenced to twenty years in prison.

Rumors about the situation abounded, including one that had the miners marching on Charleston to demand action by the legislature. The residents of Charleston were thrown into a panic, and the area around the capitol was fortified against such a possibility. The march never materialized; the reaction to it, however, was a good example of the state-of-siege mentality under which the citizens in this part of the state were living at the time.

The tension continued until March 4, 1913, when Dr. Henry D. Hatfield was inaugurated as governor. Hatfield immediately traveled to the strike area. He ordered civil rights restored to the miners, abolished the hated military courts, freed Mother Jones, and imposed peace on both sides of the conflict. The struggle along the creeks had finally come to an end.

Encampment of state militia called into Paint Creek to enforce martial law, 1912. *WVU*

Coal-company guards on Paint Creek with their pet bear, 1912. *SWV*

The remarkable collection of guns and ammunition displayed on the capitol lawn in Charleston was gathered by state troopers in the Paint Creek area after the first declaration of martial law in that county on September 2, 1912. *WVU*

PAINT CREEK SCENES

1912-13

Mine guards at Cabin Creek Junction the day before martial law was declared, September 1, 1912.

Militia detraining with a mine guard patrolling in the foreground.

Paint Creek photos from the B.E. Andre Collection.

Militia camp scene.

Militia detraining on Paint Creek.

Militia troops in camp.

Soldiers at Paint Creek.
SWV

Mary Harris "Mother" Jones, the firebrand of the coalfields in the early 1900s, was born in Cork, Ireland, in 1837. As a young woman, she taught school in Memphis, Tennessee, and worked as a dressmaker in Chicago. Her husband and children died in the Memphis yellow fever epidemic of the 1870s; it was then that she entered the labor movement, dedicating her life to improving conditions for American workers. She traveled all over the United States as a labor organizer.

Mother Jones participated in mine strikes in Colorado and West Virginia, for which she was arrested and jailed many times. In 1919, when she was almost ninety years old, she delivered a rabid speech from the state capitol steps in Charleston, calling Governor Cornwell several (unprintable) names. The Charleston *Daily Mail* referred to her as "that disreputable old woman."

A highly controversial figure, Mother Jones was even accused of working for the coal companies, often at the same time she was calling upon the miners to strike. There is no doubt, however, that she has earned a place in the history of labor reform in the United States. She died in 1931. *SWV*

Quarter-inch iron plates placed around the bed of a resident of Willis Branch, Fayette County, to ward off stray bullets. A strike begun in 1919 at Willis Branch lasted eighteen months. It led to the deaths of a number of miners and mine guards and caused the destruction of the mine camp. *WVU*

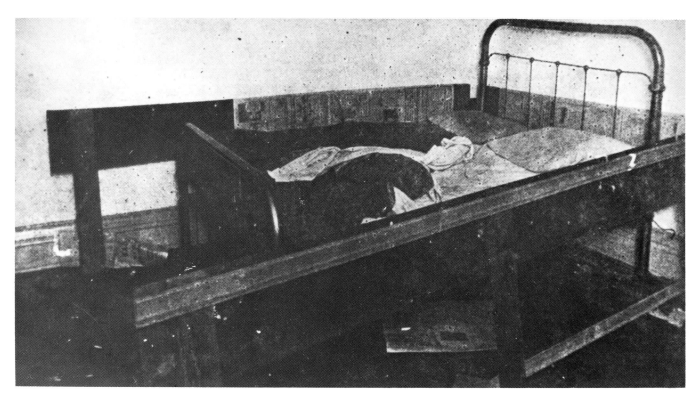

MATEWAN MASSACRE

Paint Creek and Cabin Creek were not the only scenes of violence in the southern coalfields. Mingo County, along the Tug River, was also riddled with crime and corruption. A strike was called around the town of Matewan in May 1920, with the support of the sheriff, the mayor of the town, and the chief of police. The Red Jacket Mining Company, the subject of the strike, made the decision to evict some of the strike leaders from their company-owned houses. Mine guards were hired from the Baldwin-Felts Agency to serve the eviction notices.

On May 19, twelve of the guards, led by Albert and Lee Felts, arrived at Matewan from Bluefield. They served the company's eviction orders and were standing on the main street of the town waiting for the train home. "Two Gun" Sid Hatfield, Matewan's chief of police, passed by Albert Felts and apparently without provocation shot him in the head. At that point all hell broke loose, with gunfire coming from all directions. When the firing stopped, seven guards, Mayor Testerman, and two miners lay dead. Several other "Baldwin Thugs," as the guards were called, were wounded but escaped death. The "Baldwin Thugs" were so hated that many of the local residents danced around the corpses as they lay in the street.

Hatfield and twenty-two other participants were indicted for murder. A trial was set to take place in Williamson, the county seat of Mingo County, on January 28, 1921. After nine weeks of testimony, all the defendants were acquitted, an inevitable outcome for any trial held in Mingo County. A second trial was held with a change of venue to Pocahontas County, but the verdict was no different.

The story was not to end here. The town of Mohawk, just over the line in McDowell County, was the scene of an attack; Sid Hatfield and Ed Chambers, one of the other participants in the "Matewan Massacre," were accused of the crime. It is commonly held that the actual shooting was staged by several McDowell County guards, who then accused the two men in order to force them to come across the county line, where revenge for the Matewan affair could be exacted.

On August 1, 1921, Hatfield and Chambers did go to Welch in McDowell County to make an appearance in court. They apparently did not fear any bodily harm, but as they walked up the courthouse steps a number of Baldwin-Felts mine guards who had been appointed deputy sheriffs were there to meet them. Shots were fired, and Hatfield and Chambers fell dead, as their wives watched. The guards pleaded self-defense and were acquitted months later in a trial in Welch, another miscarriage of justice in the coalfields.

Violence in "Bloody Mingo" was not limited to the events surrounding the "Matewan Massacre." In June 1920, the "Three Days' Battle of the Tug" was fought between thousands of miners and mine guards. The battle raged along an eight-mile front, ending after three days only because both sides ran out of ammunition. The number of casualties in the Battle of the Tug was never determined. In the following March, newly inaugurated Governor E.F. Morgan proclaimed martial law in the Tug Valley, sending in Major Tom B. Davis to enforce the decree. Federal troops eventually were able to stop the bloodshed.

Albert "Sid" Hatfield, chief of police of Matewan during the massacre. *WVU*

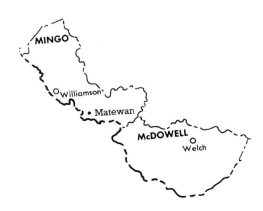

Baldwin-Felts mine guards killed in the "Matewan Massacre." Top row: C.T. Higgins; Albert Felts; Lee Felts. Bottom row: C.B. Cunningham; A.J. Booher; E.C. Powell; J.W. Ferguson.   *WVU*

Main street of Matewan, where the massacre occurred on May 19, 1920.   *WVU*

Bullet holes fired into a building during the massacre. *WVU*

Top right: "Two Gun" Sid Hatfield. Bottom right: Ed Chambers. Both were assassinated on the steps of the McDowell County Courthouse on August 1, 1921. *WVU*

McDowell County courthouse, Welch, where Hatfield and Chambers were assassinated (spot marked by "x"). *WVU*

The author standing on the site of the
fatal shooting of Hatfield and Chambers
in Welch.

Members of the "Mingo Militia" during
the 1920 battles in the Tug Valley. They
were appointed special deputy sheriffs by
the Mingo County Court and soon allied
themselves with the mine guards against
the striking miners. *SWV*

Moonshine-whiskey still apparatus confiscated from the striking miners in Mingo County. No. 1 is Judge R.D. Bailey, who tried the "Matewan Massacre" defendants. No. 2 is Major Tom B. Davis who, as acting adjutant general of West Virginia, was sent in to enforce martial law in Mingo County. *WVU*

LOGAN COUNTY AND THE ARMED MARCH

Of all the coal counties in West Virginia, none was more corrupt than Logan County. From 1913 until 1934, Don Chafin, who served first as county assessor and later as sheriff, ruled the county along with hundreds of his "special appointed" deputy sheriffs, who acted as his personal mine guards. Chafin successfully kept the UMWA out for many years, virtually controlling the lives of everyone in the county. He essentially had his own "feudal kingdom" in the heart of the coalfields.

The United Mine Workers of America had organized the mines in the Kanawha and New River fields and was determined to do the same in Logan County. In August 1919, union miners armed themselves, and over five thousand men began a march to Logan County to wrest control of the mines from Chafin and his guards. Upon the threat of federal troops made by Governor Cornwell, however, the miners disbanded. The legislature was called upon to investigate Logan County corruption, but no action was taken. As the legislature was controlled at that time by the coal companies, this came as no surprise.

By 1921 conditions had worsened in the county. The union, under the leadership of Frank Keeney, urged the miners from the 1919 march to rally at the capitol in Charleston. Mother Jones was again there, giving an inflammatory speech denouncing the governor and the coal operators. A few days later Keeney asked the miners to gather their arms and meet at Lens Creek near Marmet to begin a second march to Logan County. Their objectives: to hang Chafin, organize the mines, and liberate adjacent Mingo County from the martial law that had been imposed upon it in the wake of the violence there.

This was insurrection. Governor Morgan requested federal troops from President Warren G. Harding. General H.H. Bandholtz was sent to the scene to urge the miners to abandon their march. After he was able to enlist the help of Keeney, Bandholtz succeeded in defusing the situation.

William Blizzard

A short while later, there was an alleged attack upon a group of miners by Chafin's deputies and the state police. William Blizzard, the president of UMWA Subdistrict No. 2, organized his men and once again they headed toward Logan County. Chafin assembled his "army" to meet the miners. All the necessary ingredients were present for a genuine civil war.

The scene of battle would be Blair Mountain in Logan County, a natural barrier to access to Logan County. Chafin set up breastworks on its summit to protect his army of three thousand men. An attacking force of over three thousand miners met Chafin's army of men, and for several days a heated battle was waged, with machine guns being used on both sides. Many of the participants were veterans of World War I, and this was as real a battle as any they had fought then.

The governor again requested federal assistance. General Bandholtz brought two thousand troops and by September 3 had the situation under control. The miners were disarmed and dispersed, Chafin's men ordered back to Logan County. There were numerous casualties on both sides, but no accurate count was ever taken. In Charleston, several army bombers flown in from Washington, D.C. under the command of Brigadier General Billy Mitchell were put on alert to assist the troops if called upon. In Mitchell's words, he "would use gas if necessary." Luckily this was not to be the case.

Two of several U.S. Army Martin bombers lined up on a field at Kanawha City, Charleston. They were commanded by Brigadier General Billy Mitchell and were ordered into West Virginia for possible use against the armed miners. *B.F. Andre Collection*

Hundreds of miners and union officials were indicted and jailed. Four officials, Frank Keeney, Fred Mooney, Bill Petry, and William Blizzard, were eventually taken to Logan County and jailed to await trial. Because of local sentiment, the trials of hundreds of prisoners were moved to Jefferson County in the state's Eastern Panhandle. It was ironic that the Jefferson County Courthouse, the scene of John Brown's treason trial in 1859, would be the site for these trials.

As with other trials in the state, justice was "bent" by both sides. The county was crowded with people trying to influence prospective jurors. Blizzard was acquitted on the basis of testimony from many of his codefendants, however, one man was convicted of treason. In later years, Blizzard would become president of District 17 of the United Mine Workers of America and a powerful union leader in the state.

By this time the county was so divided in its opinions concerning the union that a fair trial was not possible for anyone. Justice was attempted by sending the defendants first to Greenbrier County and later to Fayette County, but it appeared to be impossible to obtain a fair hearing anywhere in the state. Over two years and thousands of dollars were spent without resulting in the conviction of any of the union members.

All the courtroom battles and armed conflict did not improve conditions in the coalfields, however. The union was allowed to organize in the southern coalfields only after the passage of the National Industrial Recovery Act (NIRA) in the early 1930s. Chafin was finally forced out of Logan County in 1934. He died in Huntington in 1954, leaving a large estate built almost certainly on his corrupt practices in the coalfields.

Jefferson County Courthouse in Charles Town, where the treason trial was held. *WVU*

Leaders of the march to Logan and Mingo counties. From the left: William Blizzard, president of UMWA Sub-district 2; Fred Mooney, secretary-treasurer of District 17; William Petry, vice-president of District 17, and C. Frank Keeney, president of District 17. *WVU*

Encampment of federal toops on Hewett Creek near Jeffery, Boone County, and the Blair Mountain battlefield site, September 1921. *WVU*

Freight train loaded with miners passing through Ramage, Boone County. The train had been hijacked to take the men to the foot of Blair Mountain. *WVU*

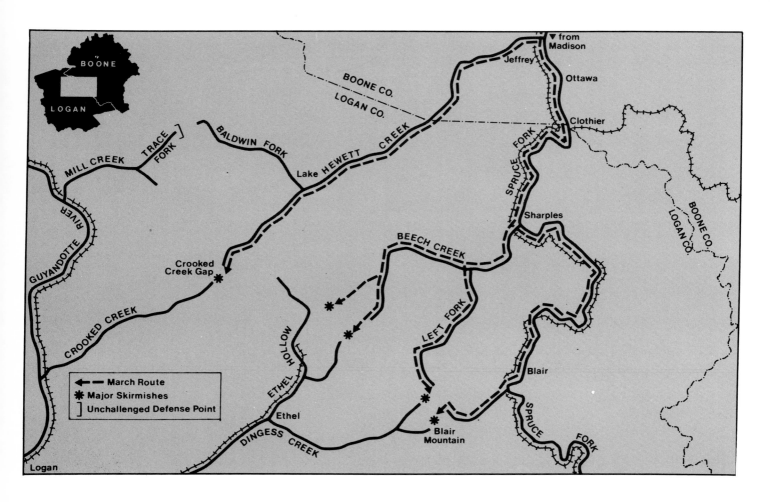

Route of the armed march and battle sites. *Courtesy* Goldenseal *magazine*

THE NORTHERN COALFIELDS

Not all the confrontations between coal operators and miners were confined to southern West Virginia. Although the mines in the northern section of the state were unionized following World War I, most of the coal companies there broke their union contracts in 1924. As a result, the state was once again embroiled in armed rebellion. The northern companies also called upon the help of the Baldwin-Felts mine guards, many of whom had gained experience in violence in the battles in the southern coalfields.

On October 10, 1924, over twenty thousand miners walked off their jobs rather than sign the yellow-dog contracts required by their employers. Scabs were brought in and the strike went on for months. Miners and their families were evicted from their company-owned homes, adding to the hatred for the scab workers.

There were no major battles between the mine guards and strikers as in the south; however, several disastrous mine explosions that killed a number of miners occurred during the four-year 1924-28 strike period. The explosions were highly suspicious, although it has never been determined if they were deliberately caused or the fault of inexperienced scab miners. The Baldwin-Felts guards were eventually ordered to leave the area, but local guards continued to evict union miners from their homes. It was only with the Great Depression of 1929 and the collapse of the coal industry that the strike was finally settled.

After 1933 and the passage of the NIRA, all the coalfields in West Virginia were unionized. This ended the extreme violence; bitter strikes continued to occur over the years, however, some lasting for several months. In recent years the decline in coal production has caused a corresponding decrease in UMWA membership. The struggle for the union today has become the attempt to maintain its position of strength in the state's coal industry.

Transportation

WE HAVE noted how the growth of the coal industry in West Virginia was virtually controlled by the development of the state's railroads. As more trackage was laid following the Civil War, there was a corresponding increase in the volume of coal mined and shipped from the state. This coincided with the rapid industrialization of the country as a whole during this period, which greatly increased the demand for coal.

The Baltimore and Ohio Railroad (B&O) was the first railroad to cross the state before the Civil War, the construction of its main line having begun in the 1840s. Its completion opened up the coalfields in the northern section of present-day West Virginia.

The Chesapeake and Ohio (C&O) reached the Ohio River in the 1870s, allowing access to the fabulously rich Kanawha and New River fields. Begun in 1881, the Norfolk and Western Railway (N&W) passed through the southern part of the state, opening up the Pocahontas and Williamson fields. The N&W provided a route to deliver southern coal to markets on the East Coast and overseas through its terminus at Norfolk, Virginia.

Scenes such as this railroad yard in Williamson, Mingo County, show the importance of "King Coal" in years past. *WVU*

Norfolk and Western LC-1 electric locomotives along the Bluestone River in southern West Virginia about 1925. These powerful locomotives were placed in service in 1915 to better cope with the steep grades in the coalfields and the problem of smoke in the tunnels. The Norfolk and Western power-generating plant was located in Bluestone and furnished eleven thousand volts of power. Of special interest in this photo are the coal cars, which were built of wood in 1918 to conserve steel for the war effort. Surprisingly durable, many survived into the 1930s. *Kanawha County Public Library*

The final railroad to penetrate the rugged mountains of southern West Virginia was the Virginian Railway. It was built to connect Deepwater, about thirty miles east of Charleston, with Matoaka in McDowell County. Both the C&O and the N&W fought the completion of the Virginian because of a fear of increased competition, but the road was finally extended to Tidewater, Virginia. With its completion in 1909, the Virginian could haul its coal all the way from the southern coalfields to the Atlantic coast on its own tracks.

Dozens of other railroads were built in the late 1800s and early 1900s to connect with these four main lines. They eventually spread to many of the creeks and hollows in the coal regions of the state that showed any promise of making a profit.

Two of the most important branch lines were the Kanawha and Michigan (K&M) and the Coal and Coke railroads. The K&M was opened in the 1890s and ran for 153 miles from Gauley Bridge to Point Pleasant and into Ohio, moving coal from the upper Kanawha Valley to the railroads serving the Midwest and Great Lakes area. It was a very profitable route and in 1910 was acquired by the C&O.

The Coal and Coke Railroad was built by Henry Gassaway Davis to provide access to his mining interests in Randolph, Upshur, Braxton, and Gilmer counties. The road finally reached Charleston in 1906. It was taken over by the B&O in 1916.

River transportation also has played a key role in the movement of coal out of West Virginia. River traffic almost came to a standstill with the expansion of the railroads. Improvements in the state's water transportation systems following World War I, however, resulted in increased volumes of coal being shipped by river, and the state's waterways are still important transportation arteries. The Kanawha and Ohio rivers provide the major routes used by river traffic today.

A small steam engine from a local coal railway pulls wooden coal cars near Crab Orchard, Raleigh County, in the early 1900s. *Author's collection*

A Mallet engine at Mt. Hope, Fayette County. These engines were also brought into West Virginia to pull the steep grades found in the state. *Author's collection*

Coal being loaded at Consolidation Coal Company's Mine No. 37 near Fairmont, Marion County. With the advent of diesel locomotive power after World War II, a large market for the state's coal disappeared. *WVU*

Great amounts of coal have been and continue to be transported on the Kanawha and Ohio rivers in West Virginia. This is the steamboat *Keystone* pushing empty coal barges on the Kanawha River in May 1943. *LC*

Disasters

W HILE COAL mining has provided work for thousands of West Virginians over the years, it has also brought great tragedy to the state. Underground mining has always been a dangerous occupation; no one can dispute this. Modern safety measures have cut down on the accident rate, it is true; even today, however, there are certain risks involved in going underground. As late as 1968, seventy-eight men were to die as the result of an explosion at No. 9 Consol Mine near Farmington in Marion County.

The tragic history of mine disasters in West Virginia started on January 21, 1886, with an explosion at the little mining town of Newburg in Preston County. At that time, thirty-nine men, some related to each other, became the first of thousands of victims to die by explosion, fire, roof falls, and other accidents that are unavoidable in this type of mining. McDowell County has had the greatest number of mine explosions over the years, followed by Fayette County. Marion County has the undesirable distinction of having had the most casualties as a result of the great Monongah tragedy.

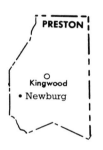

More foreign-born, new immigrants have been killed in state mining disasters than have native-born Americans. Immigrants were put to work in the mines by the thousands after 1900, often in the more dangerous occupations. More blacks than whites have lost their lives in the southern coalfields because black miners formed a higher percentage of the work force in that area of the state.

Major explosions in the coalfields can be charted to some degree by two factors: (1) the economic history of the coal industry and (2) the advancement of safety features. The first decade of the twentieth century had the largest concentration of explosions; as safety became a greater concern, disasters were scattered more evenly during succeeding decades.

In the early days of mining, the miners used open flames for their work lights, a hazard that all too frequently resulted in gas explosions. In addition, at that time no laws required the coal companies to provide "fire bosses" to check the mining areas for gas and other dangers before allowing the miners to go underground. These safety measures would be implemented later, after the cost of thousands of casualties from man-caused or natural explosions.

The need for legislation dealing with mine safety was first recognized in the late 1880s. In 1863, approximately 444,000 tons of coal were mined in West Virginia; this figure had increased to over 3 million tons by 1883. Mining accidents had risen accordingly with the growth in production, and it became obvious that regulation of some sort was necessary. The West Virginia Department of Mines was established as a watchdog agency on February 22, 1883, by the state legislature.

The first mine inspector, and the only one at that time, was Oscar A. Veazey. Veazey's duties included the inspection of all state mines, with a report to be issued annually on the conditions found and suggestions for further legislation. Since then the department has grown to ninety-seven inspectors and five district offices, with central headquarters in Charleston. The agency continues its attempts to reduce injuries and fatalities in the mines and prevent additional disasters in West Virginia's coalfields.

The U.S. Bureau of Mines was established in 1910. After the tragic 1907 Monongah explosion West Virginia coal operators petitioned Congress for the bureau. The lobbying

Ambulance No. 1 of the United States Coal and Coke Company at Gary, McDowell County, 1920. *SWV*

effort was led by William Page, G.H. Caperton and the American Mining Congress.

Of the forty-nine major disasters that have occurred since 1886, none can compare to the tragedy that befell the town of Monongah in Marion County on December 6, 1907. The largest coal mine in the northern part of the state was located there, operated by the Fairmont Coal Company, a subsidiary of the giant Consolidation Coal Company. The mines at Monongah were cut into the mountains on the west side of the West Fork River, which flowed by the town.

Many of the company's three thousand employees commuted from the nearby communities of Fairmont and Clarksburg by streetcar. A large proportion of the miners and their families were recent arrivals from Europe, looking forward to their first Christmas holiday in their new home. For many there would be no more holidays.

On December 6, three hundred miners were on duty deep in Mines No. 6 and No. 8, working the seven-foot seam of Pittsburgh coal. The exact cause of the explosion that would result in the worst underground disaster in American history has never been determined. One theory attributes it to a string of coal cars that broke loose from the train coming out of the mine, another to a "blown out shot," a defective blasting job by a miner at his coal face. Whatever the cause, the resulting explosion was so powerful that coal cars were blown out of Mine No. 8, the earth shook, and buildings in nearby towns collapsed. Even the streets of Monongah developed fissures; the whole world seemed to be in chaos. Many of the mine facilities were destroyed, some blown across the West Fork River.

With no established rescue units, volunteers poured in from surrounding mining camps. With them came hundreds of spectators from the area. It took days to dig through the debris in the two mines. A total of 361 bodies were finally removed. Many more were perhaps buried in the rubble, as no accurate records were kept of the number of men working underground at that time.

As there were no provisions then for compensating widows and children of victims, donations came from all over for the more than 250 widows and over one thousand children made fatherless by the blast. Most of the victims were from Italy, Austro-Hungary, and Russia. Only seventy-four of the casualties were native born.

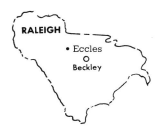

Seven years later, on April 28, 1914, the second worst mining disaster in the state's history occurred in the southern coalfields at Eccles, in Raleigh County. No. 5 Mine was the scene of that explosion, which took a total of 183 lives. It required four days for rescue workers to descend the shaft of the mine. Upon finally entering, they found total chaos. Two weeks were necessary to carry all the bodies to the earth's surface. As at Monongah, carloads of coffins had to be shipped in, and a temporary morgue was set up in the streets of the town. In this case, however, sixty-four miners in No. 6 Mine managed to survive.

The cause of the Eccles explosion was determined to be an unauthorized cutting of a barrier of coal, resulting in the disruption of the flow of air.

The third worst explosion in the state's history occurred exactly ten years to the day later, this time in the Northern Panhandle town of Benwood in Ohio County. One hundred and nineteen miners perished, with no survivors.

The list of disasters in West Virginia's coalfields could, unfortunately, continue. The rest of the stories, however, will be left to such authors as Lacy A. Dillon, who has chronicled the complete story of the state's mining tragedies in his book *They Died in the Darkness.*

A U.S. Bureau of Mines inspection car and inspectors somewhere in the West Virginia coalfields. *Author's Collection*

The Caretta first aid team, 1924, McDowell County. *SWV*

Mine rescue team with their equipment at the Coalwood mine, McDowell County, 1924. *SWV*

Students in mining engineering at West Virginia University being instructed in mine rescue work in the late 1920s. Notice the breathing apparatus and safety lights carried by each man. *SWV*

A typical mine safety meet in 1937. These events were held throughout the state for years to provide training and the exchange of ideas among the different rescue teams. *WVU*

Monument erected by the UMW to the memory of the ninety-one miners killed in the Bartley No. 1 Mine explosion on January 10, 1940.

First aid equipment used in the Bergoo Mine No. 2, Bergoo, Webster County, on display in 1946. *NA*

Remains of the fan and boiler house of Mine No. 8, Monongah, 1907.   *WVU*

Mine No. 8 entrance on December 7, one day after the great explosion.   *WVU*

Friends and relatives tried to identify the remains of the dead miners at Monongah, a grisly experience. *WVU*

With so many casualties from the Monongah disaster, a temporary morgue was set up in the city streets. *WVU*

Memorial park and statue erected at the Consolidation Coal Company park outside of Monongah, Marion County, in honor of the memory of the miners who died in the December 6, 1907, tragedy.

Fan-house fire at the Gaston mine near Fairmont, Marion County, in 1912. *WVU*

Site of a mine disaster at Barrackville, Marion County, on March 17, 1925. Wives and relatives are waiting for word on the fate of the miners. The building to the right appears to have suffered extensive damage. *WVU*

Eccles No. 5 Mine explosion in 1926 in Raleigh County.   *WVU*

Stretcher bearers bring out bodies from the Havaco No. 9 mine explosion near Welch, McDowell County, on January 15, 1946.   *SWV*

A gas explosion at Osage, Monongalia County, on May 12, 1942, killed fifty-six miners. *WVU*

The Pursglove, Monongalia County, explosion on July 9, 1942, killed twenty miners. *WVU*

STATE OF WEST VIRGINIA
DEPARTMENT OF MINES
CHARLESTON

COAL MINE FATALITIES

JOHN FLOWERS—
West Virginia Coal and Coke Corporation, Earling Mine,
Earling, Logan County, West Virginia.

Polish, Coal Loader, Age 36.
Injured Monday, February 28, 1944, 1:35 P. M.
Died Monday, February 28, 1944, 2:30 P. M.
Experience: Total unknown—At last job 3 years.

Flowers was injured fatally by a fall of roof at the face of an open-end
pillar place. The fall consisted of bone coal that had been left to protect the roof and was 10' by 13' by 6" to 9" thick. Two safety posts
had been set across the face and two rows of line posts had been set
at intervals of four feet along the left side. The place was being
worked, hand mining, by two men. Flowers was working between the
rows of line posts, using his pick, when the bone coal fell. The handle
of the pick was forced through the lower part of his chest cavity by
the fall.

JOE E. ADKINS—
Guyan Eagle Coal Company, Guyan Eagle No. 1 Mine,
Amherstdale, Logan County, West Virginia.

American, Shotfirer, Age 35.
Injured Saturday, March 11, 1944, 10:00 P. M.
Died Sunday, March 12, 1944, 5:00 P. M.
Experience: Total unknown—At last job 2 months.

Adkins received injuries, from a fall of slate at the working face,
from which he died later. Three drill holes, at the face of a room being driven, had been charged and tamped. He had fired two of the
shots. When he went back to the face to connect the third shot, he
was struck by a piece of draw slate that fell causing the injuries.
The slate was 10' by 7' by about 4" thick at the heavy end.

WILLIAM HOWARD SMITH—
Christopher Coal Company, Christopher No. 3 Mine,
Osage, Monongalia County, West Virginia.

American, Motorman, Age 34.
Injured Tuesday, March 7, 1944, 10:20 P. M.
Died Tuesday, March 7, 1944, 11:30 P. M.
Experience: Total 19 years, 1 month—At last job 4 months.

Smith was injured when his locomotive collided with a stalled trip.
The preceding trip of fourteen loads was stalled on a grade on its
way to the outside on the main haulage when the motor pinion
stripped. When the trip stalled the brakeman left the rear and went
up to the motor to find the trouble instead of going back to flag on-
coming trips. Smith had left the junction thirteen minutes behind
and was following with seven loads when his locomotive collided
with the rear car of the stalled trip. He had jumped off and was
found between the first and second car of his trip. He died on the
way to the hospital.

SAMUEL DARNELL—
Guy Hall Coal Company, Coombs Mine,
Morgantown, Monongalia County, West Virginia.

American, Coal Loader, Age 65.
Killed instantly Monday, March 13, 1944, 7:30 A. M.
Experience: Total 32 years—At last job 18 years.

Darnell was instantly killed by a fall of bone coal on the entry at a
room switch. He, with the mine foreman and another man, had
found this roof "working." While they were preparing to set safety
posts in order to take the roof down, it began to fall. Darnell became confused and ran directly under the fall.

CARL SHAFFER—
Davis Coal and Coke Company, No. 40 Mine,
Pierce, Tucker County, West Virginia.

American, Timberman, Age 35.
Injured Wednesday, March 8, 1944, 9:45 A. M.
Died Wednesday, March 8, 1944, 10:30 P. M.
Experience: Total 2 years, 5 months—At last job 2 years, 5 months.

While coupling cars Shaffer was crushed between a loaded car and
crossbar. He had been engaged in cleaning up coal that had accumu-
lated about a door on the heading. The car he was loading had been
switched to a nearby spur to allow a trip to pass. He was injured
while coupling this car to the trip to have it replaced at the door.
The clearance between the top of the car and the crossbar was only
seven inches.

EARL BROWN—
Princess Dorothy Coal Company, Eunice No. 2 Mine,
Eunice, Raleigh County, West Virginia.

American, Car Coupler, Age 40.
Injured Wednesday, March 8, 1944, 11:15 P. M.
Died Thursday, March 9, 1944, 4:30 P. M.
Experience: Total 13 years—At last job 1 month.

This accident occurred at the foot of the incline on the outside.
Brown was struck and rolled by cars while attempting to couple
empties onto the rope. As he was about to make the coupling the motor
pushed another trip against the empties. In attempting to escape,
it is thought he slipped and fell against the cars and was rolled
causing injuries from which he died.

VINNIE E. BLEVINS—
Sterling Smokeless Coal Company, Sterling Mine,
Whitby, Raleigh County, West Virginia.

American, Scraper Man, Age 25.
Injured Thursday, February 24, 1944, 8:40 A. M.
Died Thursday, February 24, 1944, 2:30 P. M.
Experience: Total 6 years—At last job 4 months.

Blevins was fatally injured by being crushed against posts by a conveyor scraper. The view from the hoist to tail jack was obstructed
and as no signal system was used, the operator depended on contact
of scraper against tail jack as the signal for stopping. When the
empty scraper was returned to the face it dislodged the tail jack
which caused the scraper to be pulled toward the line sheave. As
Blevins was working in the space between the tail jack and the line
jack, he was caught and crushed against a post.

GEORGE F. KERR—
Century Coal Company, Century No. 1 Mine,
Century, Barbour County, West Virginia.

American, Coal Loader, Age 69.
Injured Saturday, February 26, 1944, 12:30 A. M.
Died Thursday, March 9, 1944, 11:30 A. M.
Experience: Total 15 years—At last job 2 years.

The injury was caused by a fall of roof at the face of an entry being
driven. A crossbar had been set within three feet of the face. Eight
tons of coal had been loaded from the center of the cut and a safety
post had been set in this space. It had been set near a fissure in the
roof but, evidently, the cap piece did not span the fissure. Kerr was
digging at the right side, his buddy shoveling from the left side of
the working place. His buddy noticed the roof begin to fall, but not
in time to give sufficient warning. Kerr received injuries from which
he died several days later. The size of the rock was about 3' by 5'
by 1' in thickness. The place had been examined thirty minutes before and pronounced safe.

A grim reminder of the hazards of underground mining.   *SWV*

Coal miner at Welch, 1946. *LC*

Living Conditions

COAL MINING has been and continues to be dangerous work. It is a unique occupation that breeds a certain type of individual, and generations of miners have grown up knowing no other life than the coal mines. This has changed in recent times, but it was not too many years ago that one could be "trapped" in the coalfields for life.

Much has been written throughout the years about the living conditions of the miners and their families in West Virginia. Conditions varied considerably over time and region across the state; therefore, no one term can describe them all. The image most frequently depicted in the media has been that of the miner and his family living in a tar-paper shack with little to eat. This picture, with its stigma of Appalachian poverty, has been a hard one to combat, especially in West Virginia. Certainly terrible poverty did exist at one time and, to a lesser extent, can still be found, but the quality of life has improved a great deal for most West Virginians. The state and its residents continue to suffer in some degree, however, from "bad press."

The opening up of the coalfields brought an influx of miners from the southern United States and from Europe, creating crowded, unsanitary conditions in the coal camps. The isolation of the camps only worsened the situation with the lack of modern sanitation facilities and adequate health care. The foreign-born workers often could not speak or understand English and were not use   to mining work. Deaths in the camps were numerous and frequent.

Many of the coal companies, motivated solely by greed, ignored the plight of the miners. In too many instances, the miners were treated as slave labor, tied to the company through company-owned houses and the company-store system. It was only through the efforts of the union that this type of worker-employer relationship, a throwback to feudal times in Europe, was ended.

Private property owners who found a little coal on their land would often mine it themselves and sell it along the road. This photo was taken in 1938. *LC*

Living conditions were extremely hard for the miners and their families during the depression years. The stigma of "depressed Appalachia" took many years to change. This is a disabled miner and his family in Pursglove, Monongalia County, in 1938. *LC*

It is only fair to note, however, that there were a number of coal operators who realized the importance of providing clean, healthy environments for their workers. There were coal towns with adequate health facilities, proper sanitation, schools, and community activities; not all were the desolate, grim places to live that are the most frequently portrayed. Recreation was often available in many forms, including bands and orchestras to join for those miners and their family members interested in music. Theaters, pool halls, school activities and various sports, much the same as could be found in any small town in America, were avialable in most coal towns.

One of the most popular recreational events in the coal towns up to World War II was baseball. Every town had a team, and leagues were formed throughout each region. (As there was still segregation at that time, there were both white and black teams and leagues.) Sunday was the big day in the towns, for that was when visiting teams came to play. After the war, however, baseball lost its great popularity.

An unemployed
bachelor miner at Jere,
Monongalia County, in
1937. *NA: Lewis Hine
Collection*

A Hungarian immi-
grant and his wife at
Calumet, 1935. Then
sixty-three and out of
work, he had worked in
the mines for thirty-four
years. *LC*

As noted, the depres-
sion hit the state's coalfields especially hard.
Here unemployed min-
ers are receiving their
relief checks, December
23, 1936, at Jere,
Monongalia County.
*NA: Lewis Hine Collec-
tion*

A favorite playground for the children was often around the mine tipples. Pursglove, Monongalia County, 1938. *LC*

Life during the Depression was not completely bleak. There was entertainment, and facilities were built for schools and libraries. These photos were taken at Scott's Run in the mid-1930s. *NA: Lewis Hine Collection*

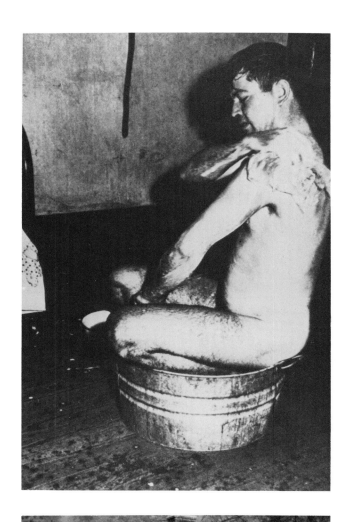

Top Right: Fifty-six years a miner when this photo was taken many years ago. *WVU*

Top Left: "Saturday night bath" in a miner's home. Indoor plumbing was a luxury few miners could afford in the 1930s and even into the 1940s. *WVU*

Bottom: Obtaining water from a well at the Wymar mine of the Wyatt Coal Company in Sharon, Kanawha County, 1946. *NA*

A Polish miner from Capels, McDowell County, 1938. *LC*

Payday, Stirrat, Logan County, 1938. *LC*

Payday at Osage, Monongalia County, 1938. *LC*

A miner checking the daily company work sheets to see the number of tons of coal he loaded during his shift. He might also be finding out if he was to work the next day. Capels, McDowell County, 1938. *LC*

A typical miner's house at Wyatt, Harrison County, 1909. *WVU*

Typical living conditions in many mining camps in the early years of the industry. *WVU*

Main street of the mining community of Chaplin, Monongalia County, 1938. *LC*

Immigrant coal miners gathering in Fayette County in the early 1900s. Once the coalfields were opened by the railraods, great numbers of men and their families were enticed to come from Europe to work. Every European nationality was eventually represented.   *SWV*

Foreign-born miners receiving instruction, possibly in the English language.   *WVU*

A truck brings food supplies to the abandoned mining town of Jere, Monongalia County, in 1938. The Great Depression hit the mining areas especially hard.   *LC*

Bargain day on Holden's main street. Since many of the coal towns were fairly isolated, with poor roads leading in and out, many business firms in the larger cities sent out trucks to sell their goods directly to the miners and their families. Better roads, mail-order catalogs, and more affluent miners eventually brought this type of retailing to a halt.   *WVU*

Music was an important part of the lives of the miners and their families. Many coal company employees formed their own bands for parades and concerts. Top: The No. 11 Mine Hungarian band at Gary, McDowell County, in 1920. Bottom: The union band at Monongah, Marion County.   *SWV*

The New River Company employees' band from MacDonald, Fayette County.   *SWV*

Recreation facilities were built in some of the coal towns for the miners and their families. Top: A poolroom at Gary, McDowell County, in 1920. Right: The interior of the Elbert, McDowell County, theater in 1935. *SWV*

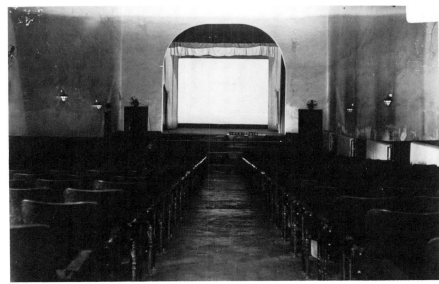

Sports were also an important part of a town's social activities. Baseball was the most popular game, and nearly every mining town had a team either in a county, United Mine Workers, or black league. The larger towns even had professional teams in minor league ball. *WVU*

Miners used whatever they could for shelter during the depression years. Here an outdoor toilet has been made from a car body and a truck made into a house. Scott's Run, Monongalia County, 1937. *NA: Lewis Hine Collection*

Promotion

This tall tower built of coal was displayed as West Virginia's exhibit at the 1907 Jamestown Exposition in Virginia. *WVU*

A coal company float, possibly in a Cincinnati parade.
*Amherst Industries
via Todd Hanson Collection*

Demonstration of the
properties of West Vir-
ginia's low-volatile
bituminous coal to a
Boston, Massachusetts,
audience in the 1920s.
The state's high-quality
coal was being shipped
all over the world by
this time. *SWV*

Another promotion for
West Virginia's leading
product. *SWV*

Several movies have
been produced through
the years on mining, the
family life of the miners,
and strife in the coal-
fields. This 1935 movie
entitled *Black Fury* was
advertised at a Morgan-
town theater. *LC*

The Legacy of Coal

NEARLY EVERY West Virginian is affected in some way by the state's coal industry. Coal is burned as fuel and used to produce electricity. Many residents earn their livings by mining or by employment in peripheral businesses. One can experience coal's impact on the state simply by driving through the northern or southern coalfields.

Many of the uses of coal are well known. As noted, most of the electricity used in West Virginia is produced by burning coal. Coke made from the state's low ash and sulphur content coal has been utilized in the production of steel. Coke-oven gas, a by-product of coke, has also been used as a fuel. There are other uses for these gases as well, and a large industry has evolved to produce a multitude of everyday products such as plastics, drugs, paints, solvents, explosives, and rubber. The conversion of coal to gasoline is also now possible. The technique has, in fact, been available for many years but has yet to be made economically feasible.

Technology continues to uncover new uses for coal; the potential for the mineral seems virtually limitless. With the storehouse of wealth to be found in the West Virginia hills, the state's coal industry is surely a giant that will once again be awakened.

Entrance to the Beckley Exhibition Coal Mine at New River Park in Beckley, Raleigh County. A one-time working coal mine can be viewed, along with a coal museum and a magnificent display of over one hundred hand-carved wooden figurines that depict the legendary John Henry and the construction of the Big Bend Tunnel.

Miner's hat and various mining lamps.

An early example of rescue equipment.

A miner's hat, electric light, goggles, lunch pail, and knee pads.

An apparatus used in the early days to transport the miners to the coal face. Built like a scooter, it was placed on a rail, and the miner would push it along with one knee on the board. His lunch pail always accompanied him.

A large collection of miners' lamps, hats, and fuel containers dating back over one hundred years is on display at the Beckley Exhibition Coal Mine Museum at New River Park.

Opposite: Artifacts in the Beckley Exhibition Coal Mine Museum at New River Park.

Monument to Joseph L. Beury at Quinnimont, Fayette County. Beury was an early coal baron, the first to ship New River coal in 1873. *NPS*

One use of coal has been in the construction of several buildings around the state. Top: The Tug Valley Chamber of Commerce building in Williamson, Mingo County. In 1933, this building was constructed of sixty-five tons of local coal. It has been placed on the National Register of Historic Places. Bottom: The "Coal House" along Route 60, just east of White Sulphur Springs, Greenbrier County. It was built in 1959 using thirty tons of cannel coal. The blocks were shaped with a hatchet and cemented with black mortar. It presently is used as a gift shop.   Top: *Historic Preservation Unit, Charleston;* Bottom: *Author's collection*

This once-magnificent brick structure at Elkhorn, McDowell County, was built as a company store by the Pocahontas Fuel Company in the World War I era. Many buildings similar to this were built in the company's mining areas to serve their employees.

Abandoned town and coal mine ruins are evident in the New River Gorge area of Fayette County. In its heyday the area was a tremendous source of coal. *All photos courtesy NPS*

Beury company store ruins.

House ruins at Caperton. The mines in this area were once owned by Queen Victoria of England.

Mine car on the track at the bottom of the tie line that brought coal down to the tipple at Kaymoor.

Mine opening at Kaymoor.

Abandoned tipple at Kaymoor.

Headhouse at
Kaymoor.

Tipple and remains of
coke ovens at
Kaymoor.

Tipple ruins at
Sewell.

Ruins of the chimney at the Sewell company office.

Ruins of the vault in the old company office at Sewell.

Powerhouse remains at the abandoned town of Fire Creek.

Tipple at
Nuttallburg.

Conveyor at Nuttall-
burg, used to bring the
coal down to the
tipple.

Old mine motor at
the abandoned town of
Nuttallburg.

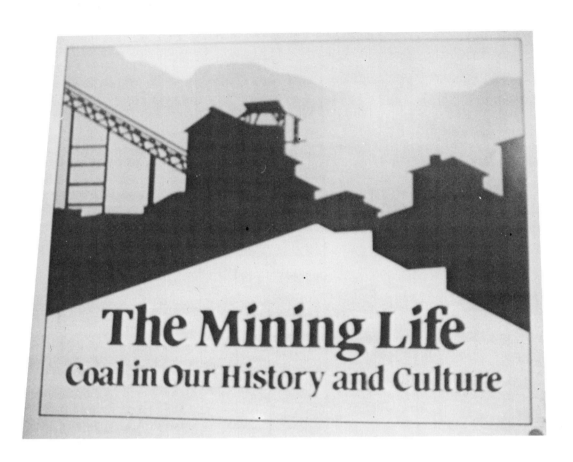

THE MINING LIFE: COAL IN OUR HISTORY AND CULTURE. A traveling exhibition sponsored by The Humanities Foundation of West Virginia, The National Endowment for The Humanities, The West Virginia Department of Culture and History and The Claude Worthington Benedum Foundation.

A miner's tent on display.

COAL PRODUCTS TREE

Showing the products obtainable from coal by carbonization in the modern by-product coke oven

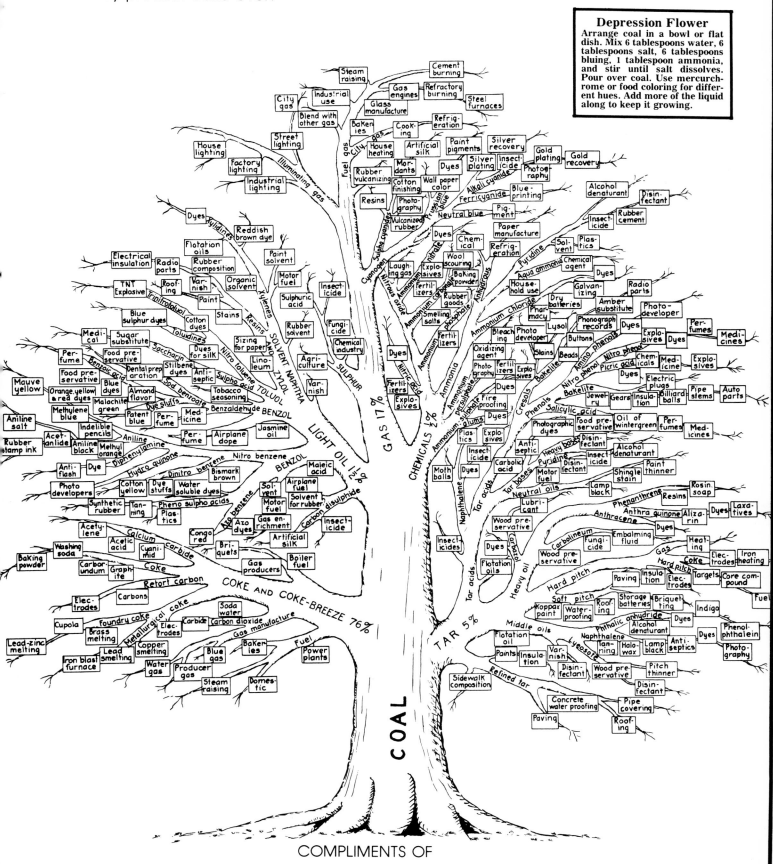

Depression Flower
Arrange coal in a bowl or flat dish. Mix 6 tablespoons water, 6 tablespoons salt, 6 tablespoons bluing, 1 tablespoon ammonia, and stir until salt dissolves. Pour over coal. Use mercurchrome or food coloring for different hues. Add more of the liquid along to keep it growing.

COMPLIMENTS OF

BECKLEY POST-HERALD   The Raleigh Register

BIBLIOGRAPHY

Conley, Phil, *History of the West Virginia Coal Industry*, Education Foundation, Inc., Charleston, W.Va., 1960.

Cross, A.T., *Report of Investigations #10, The Geology of Pittsburgh Coal*, W.Va. Geological & Economic Survey, Morgantown, W.Va., 1952 & 1971.

Dillon, Lacy, *They Died in the Darkness*, McClain Printing Co., Parsons, W.Va., 1976.

Dix, Keith, *Work Relations in the Coal Industry: The Hand-Loading Era, 1880-1930*, West Virginia University, Morgantown, W.Va., 1977.

Lane, Winthrop, *Civil War in West Virginia, A Story of the Industrial Conflict in the Coal Mines*, Arno Press, N.Y., 1969.

Lee, Howard B., *Bloodletting in Appalachia*, McClain Printing Co., Parsons, W.Va., 1969.

Mooney, Fred, *Struggle in the Coal Fields, The Autobiography of Fred Mooney*, West Virginia University, Morgantown, W.Va., 1967.

Tams, W.P., Jr., *The Smokeless Coal Fields of West Virginia: A Brief History*, West Virginia University Press, Morgantown, W.Va., 1983.

Various publications of the W.Va. Geological and Economic Survey, Morgantown, W.Va.

West Virginia Geological & Economic Survey, Volume XIII (A), *Characteristics of Minable Coal of West Virginia*, Morgantown, W.Va., 1955.

The author with an auger from the coal museum, Beckley Exhibition Coal Mine.

ABOUT THE AUTHOR

Stan Cohen is a native of Charleston and a 1961 Graduate of West Virginia University with a B.S. Degree in Geology. After working as a geologist in the oil fields and with the U.S. Forest Service, Cohen spent fifteen years in various businesses in Montana. In 1976 he established Pictorial Histories Publishing Company; since then he has written or co-authored sixty-six books and published over two hundred titles. He now divides his time between Montana and Charleston, maintaining offices in both locations.

Other books by the author are *A Pictorial Guide to West Virginia's Civil War Sites: and Related Information*; *The Civil War in West Virginia — A Pictorial History*; and *Historic Springs of the Virginias — A Pictorial History*.